DON'T BOUNCE BACK
REBUILD FORWARD

*How to Reclaim Your Power
When Life Breaks the Script*

DON'T BOUNCE BACK
REBUILD FORWARD

*How to Reclaim Your Power
When Life Breaks the Script*

ANDREA GASH

Niche Press
Indianapolis, IN

DON'T BOUNCE BACK, **REBUILD FORWARD**
How to Reclaim Your Power When Life Breaks the Script

Copyright © 2026 by Andrea Gash

All rights reserved. No part of this book may be used or reproduced in any manner whatsoever without prior written consent of the author, except as provided by the United States of America copyright law.

For permission to reprint portions of this content or bulk purchases, contact andrea@andreagash.com.

Author Photograph by: Emily Stewart, Dirt Darlin'

Published by Niche Press: NichePress.com
Indianapolis, IN

ISBN
Hardcover: 978-1-970329-10-0
Paperback: 978-1-970329-11-7
eBook: 978-1-970329-12-4

Library of Congress Control Number: 2026902827

The views expressed herein are solely those of the author and do not necessarily reflect the views of the publisher.

Dedicated to my parents — all of them:

Mike and Lisa Masterson
Bob and Pat Chapman
Vern and Jan Gash

Each of you shaped every chapter of who I am.
Thank you for everything.

A hand-up is one of the most powerful ways to help someone reach their destination — achieving their goals in their own way and on their own time. Andrea Gash offers a hand-up through her own experience and journey, guiding you as you navigate your path.

When the world feels overwhelming and chaotic, *Don't Bounce Back, Rebuild Forward* is a reminder of the power you already have and gives you the framework to move forward at your own pace without losing your individuality or compromising your values.

— **RAFAEL SANCHEZ,** *Anchor/Reporter, Fox 59/CBS 4*

This beautiful work captures the tender, disorienting space between who we were and who we're becoming. The Momentum Method doesn't push you forward; it gently walks with you, reminding you that momentum can start with even the smallest breath of self-trust.

— **MOXXY SCHOEFFLER,** *Director, Role-Based Learning, Salesforce*

Having personally encountered significant life changes — battling thyroid cancer, experiencing divorce, and navigating career transitions, *Don't Bounce Back, Rebuild Forward* deeply resonated with me. Andrea Gash highlights the courage required to embrace change and the steps needed to move ahead. My own search for purpose taught me that new beginnings matter more than revisiting the past. This book is an inspiring read for anyone ready to pause, reflect on who they are in the moment, and step confidently into their future.

— **MELISSA KLOSTER,** *Corporate Communications Leader*

Andrea Gash offers a grounded, relatable perspective on a challenge many of us face, especially those of us who have followed the traditional script of working hard and building a "good" life, only to find ourselves unfulfilled when our script breaks.

Andrea provides clear, practical steps to help you write a new script, one that reflects who you are now and the life you truly want to create.

— **NOELLE GUNN ELLIOTT,** *Marketing and Communications Specialist, Creator and Producer of* The Mamalogues

Life does not always go as planned. I discovered this firsthand after getting life-altering medical diagnoses for both my husband and me. *Don't Bounce Back, Rebuild Forward* puts into words the grief and anger I've felt since that moment five years ago and then provides a blueprint for how to create momentum while learning to accept and own those things we cannot change.

We can't go backward, so Andrea outlines how we can go forward.

— **KELLI WARD,** *Director of Corporate Social Responsibility, Aventiv Technologies*

Contents

FOREWORD	The Courage to Begin Again	xi
PREFACE	Before the Rebuild	xiii
INTRO	Don't Bounce Back, Rebuild Forward	1
PART ONE	**WHEN THE SCRIPT BREAKS**	**7**
CHAPTER 1	When Life Breaks the Script	9
CHAPTER 2	Not Starting Over, Rebuilding Forward	21
CHAPTER 3	Living in the Aftermath	29
PART TWO	**THE MOMENTUM METHOD**	**45**
CHAPTER 4	Step 1 – Hit Reset	47
CHAPTER 5	Step 2 – Call It What It Is	57
CHAPTER 6	Step 3 – Get Back to You	69
CHAPTER 7	Step 4 – Dare to Dream	81
CHAPTER 8	Step 5 – Rewrite Your Script	93
PART THREE	**THE WORK OF LIVING AGAIN**	**107**
CHAPTER 9	Life Interrupted	109
CHAPTER 10	Finding Your Way Back	117
CHAPTER 11	Measure Your Life by Meaning	125
CHAPTER 12	Where Ritual Meets Healing	131
PART FOUR	**REBUILD FORWARD**	**143**
CHAPTER 13	Living Your Values	145
CHAPTER 14	Rebuilding That Works for You	153
CHAPTER 15	You Don't Have to Go Back to Who You Were Before	163
Endnotes		171
Acknowledgements		175
About Andrea Gash		177

FOREWORD

The Courage to Begin Again

I first met Andrea Gash at an event in 2015 and was immediately impressed by her intellect, poise, and enthusiasm. We connected effortlessly, and when she asked me to become her mentor, I felt honored. What I didn't realize was how much she would give back. Her energy and insight lifted me up as much as my guidance supported her.

As an executive coach, I work with many people who are struggling through significant challenges — burnout, job loss, divorce, or even the death of a loved one. In these moments, society tells us to power through, suck it up, and move on.

While that is the default script many of us follow, Andrea's method defies these perpetual messages we get from society. She explains how you don't need to bounce back from a disruption. You are not the same person after everything has changed. Instead, you can give yourself the gift of rebuilding forward. Andrea taught me that when she helped me after my script shattered.

My overachieving work ethic led to illness, exhaustion, a crisis of career faith, and ultimately, burnout. Instead of capitulating to the anxiety, overwhelm, and disconnection associated with burnout, Andrea helped me rewrite my script and hit reset. I rebuilt and redesigned my life and career to truly honor my values. I can even hear Andrea's calm voice in my mind when she explains how momentum isn't about how fast you get there; it's about the direction you take.

Andrea's signature Momentum Method helped me get to where I am now, and it can help you. She details a clear path and powerful tools to help navigate the unknown. She also shares her personal script-breaking stories in thoughtful, vulnerable, and courageous ways, providing a playbook for doing things differently. Andrea's experience shows how you can break away from what you did in the past so that you can rebuild stronger, clearer, and truer than ever before.

With *Don't Bounce Back, Rebuild Forward*, Andrea eloquently details her expertise, compassion, and strategies, providing the tools and knowledge to help you navigate life's disruptions and script breaks. Andrea has found the courage again and again to rebuild her life and career after many unexpected changes, and now, she shares that with you.

This book will help you understand that you are not alone and that the life you imagined can be attained. Momentum starts, not in bouncing back, but in choosing to rebuild forward.

— **CAROLINE DOWD-HIGGINS,**
Speaker, Executive Coach, Author, Media Host

PREFACE

Before the Rebuild

I decided to write this book after my mother-in-law, Jan, unexpectedly died in my arms as I tried to perform CPR. It was the final straw in a long season of loss and unraveling. By my early forties, I had lost my biological parents, my adopted parents, and my in-laws. I faced infertility, caregiving, and major identity shifts that made me question who I was and what was left of the life I'd imagined.

In the aftermath of each loss, I did what I thought I was supposed to do. I smiled, worked hard, showed up, and pushed forward, never letting the cracks show. I wrote obituaries and thank you notes, planned funerals, and then went back to work. I looked polished and professional, meeting goals and deadlines, but inside, I was shattered. My script was broken.

Eventually, pretending stopped working. For me, there wasn't a breakdown, just a quiet unraveling and a voice that kept whispering, *I can't keep living like this.*

That's when rebuilding began, piece by piece. Over time, I began to see a pattern — there were five steps that helped me regain momentum when I had none. I called these steps the Momentum Method.

I hope that this book meets you where you are, whether it's right after a script break, at the beginning of your unraveling, or somewhere in the middle.

You don't have to go back to who you were before; you can rebuild forward.

Andrea

INTRODUCTION

Don't Bounce Back, Rebuild Forward

There are moments in life that divide life into *before* and *after*.

I call these script breaks, and they're life disruptions that come in many forms. Sometimes it's a loss you never saw coming, such as a death, a diagnosis, or a betrayal. Other times, it's the slow unraveling of a marriage or a career that no longer fits. It can be the baby you thought you'd have, but didn't, a dream that never turned out, or realizing your life isn't what you thought it would be. If you've ever been the one quietly holding it together while your life fell apart, or you are standing in the middle of a life upheaval, this book is for you.

Often, it isn't a single event that breaks you; there's just one that finally cracks open what was already fragile. I know because I have lived through more than one script break myself.

This book won't rush you past the pain or provide easy fixes. Instead, it will help you make sense of what's happening, find steadier footing on hard days, and start rebuilding a life that suits who you are now after everything has changed.

THE BREAK

It was a Friday in June, and I had taken the day off work to spend with my husband, Justin. It was around 10:00 a.m., and we were watching the show *Call the Midwife*, and like I always did, I had tried to call my mom several times. We talked every day, usually more than once, and I'd been checking in with her more often since my dad had passed away just seven months earlier.

When she didn't answer, I worried a little bit, but she'd been tired lately, and I thought maybe she was sleeping in. I wish I lived closer than three hours away. Two days earlier, she'd been to her doctor and received a clean bill of health.

When the phone rang, and I saw her number on the caller ID, I picked up and joked, "How late were you going to sleep in today?"

On the other end was my brother's voice. His tone told me everything before his words did.

"Andi," he said quietly. "I found Mom this morning. She's gone."

AFTER

There's a moment after loss when noise stops. The world keeps moving, but you can't. You're standing in the middle of what used to be your life, surrounded by pieces that no longer fit together.

My experiences led me to write this book: the loss of my biological parents, adopted parents, and in-laws; infertility; caretaking; and identity shifts. Each one chipped away at the life I had imagined, though I refused to admit it at the time. I had perfected the art of masking, smile on, high-functioning, even when my heart was shattered.

I thought that's what society expected of me. We reward resilience, hustle, and "getting back to normal." So that's what I did... until I couldn't anymore.

What I learned throughout my rebuilding journey is that you can never go back to the way things were, because you are different. You have to rebuild from where you are.

To rebuild, I followed five steps. They weren't created by psychologists or professors; they were born from my own unraveling and the slow work of rebuilding. I later called it the Momentum Method.

STEP 1: Hit Reset
▶ It's time to pause, stop trying to bounce back, and allow yourself to breathe and begin again.

STEP 2: Call It Like It Is
▶ You have permission to talk honestly about what happened and how you feel without sugarcoating it. Honestly breaks the illusion of control and gives shape to what you've lost.

STEP 3: Get Back to You
▶ Reconnect with who you are underneath the roles, responsibilities, and expectations, and get back to what matters to *you.*

STEP 4: Dare to Dream
▶ When you've been through the worst, imagining something new takes courage, but this is where possibility returns.

STEP 5: Rewrite Your Script
▶ Begin designing a life that reflects who you are now, not who you were before.

Rebuilding isn't about restoring what was, but rediscovering who you are now. The Momentum Method is a guide to help you navigate loss and change. These steps aren't linear. You'll sometimes move backward; we all do. You have permission to follow them in any order, repeat as needed, and even create your own.

If you are currently going through, or have already lived through, a painful script break, you are not alone. I know what it's like to wear the mask of composure while unraveling inside.

You're not starting over. You're beginning again, with wisdom and grace you didn't have before.

You can't go back and change the beginning,
but you can start where you are and change the ending.
—C.S. LEWIS

REFLECTION

Throughout the book, you'll find reflection exercises that will gently guide you through your own rebuilding process. Keep your favorite mug close, and have a notebook and pen nearby, but most of all, bring your honesty. That's the part that will move this work from the page and into your life.

PART ONE

WHEN THE SCRIPT BREAKS

CHAPTER 1

When Life Breaks the Script

*Life happens not in brightness or darkness,
but in the average light of an ordinary day.*

—UNKNOWN

Most of us build our lives around a script. It's that picture in our mind of how things are supposed to go: marriage, children, career success, financial stability, a long life surrounded by those you love. We build our calendars, our dreams, and even our identities around the script we've written. My script included getting married, having children, and watching my parents and my husband's parents spoil them. I imagined all the holidays we would spend together as a family.

Then comes the script break.

DEFINING THE SCRIPT BREAK

A script break is when life takes a turn you didn't plan for and didn't want. Sometimes it happens in an instant, with a phone call or diagnosis. Other times, it creeps in slowly, through years of unraveling, until you hardly recognize the life you are living. Either way, it shakes the foundation upon which you've built everything.

You may have already experienced a script break. Perhaps it was the death of someone you never thought you would live without or a divorce you never imagined would happen. Maybe it was a job loss, a frightening diagnosis, a long stretch of burnout that left you exhausted, or the quiet burn of realizing you no longer recognize yourself.

Some common script breaks include:

- Job loss
- Identity shift
- Diagnosis
- Death
- Caregiving
- Burnout
- Divorce
- Chronic Illness

If you see your story on that list — or if your break looks different but feels just as shattering — know that you are not alone.

Every script break is different, but the shock of realizing this wasn't the plan is universal.

Many of my script breaks were personal, but underlying those challenges was the slow realization that my jobs didn't challenge or excite me, while speaking before an audience and helping others did. In fact, years ago, I even started developing a speaking career plan, but then COVID hit, and we adopted our son. It seemed other priorities always got in the way.

But I kept coming back to the feeling of excitement I had while speaking. I loved the thrill of creating and researching a new keynote, tailoring it to an audience, and making space for small-group discussion. I loved helping people; it truly gave me purpose.

When your script breaks, it can feel like your story is over. Yet, what if instead of the end, it's a turning point and a chance to find your purpose?

A script break is never easy. You'll likely feel uncertainty, grief, fear, and many other feelings. To navigate these moments, I developed the Momentum Method. It starts at the beginning and helps you rebuild forward when life doesn't go as planned. Each step helps you reclaim who you are at that moment and provides tools and strategies to help you begin again. The goal is not simply to return to your old life, but rather to construct a new life that aligns with who you are *now*.

Whether your disruption was sudden or slow, devastating or disorienting, this book will help you find your footing and gather the courage to write your next chapter.

A Quiet Unraveling

My script break began in mid-January, my least favorite time of year. The Christmas tree had been taken down, and the world felt cold without the glow of twinkling lights. The week before, my mother-in-law, Jan, a second mother to me, had died in my arms unexpectedly.

I was sitting on the floor of her home, going through her items one by one. I was surrounded by bags and boxes, separated into trash, donations, keep, and friends. I was in her kitchen, her favorite room, going through her baking supplies, and I stopped when I picked up her favorite cake plate. It was the one she used every holiday and for our birthday cakes. Jan was a talented baker and had given me many of her recipes over the years. As I went through her baking pans, I could almost smell her sugar cookies, a family favorite, especially during the holidays. I cried until my body ached and tears ran down my face, hitting the floor. I cried for what we had had and what was lost.

A few days later, after taking my allowed three days of bereavement, I was back to work, hair and makeup done, a smile plastered on my face. I went into the day with a "fake it till you make it" mindset, but soon realized that was easy because hardly anyone mentioned what had happened. Only a few close work friends acknowledged my grief and offered words of support.

The silence of my colleagues was deafening. I had a meeting on my first day back, and although they all knew what had happened, it wasn't mentioned. I felt alone and unacknowledged. I have always been one to reach out and check in with others; in fact, that's something I pride myself on. Instead of anyone asking how I was, I was asked about an upcoming deadline and asked to schedule a meeting.

I felt bitter and resentful, a major shift from my normally upbeat and positive attitude. I felt abandoned, alone, and numb. I had undoubtedly been through losses before, but this felt different. I had already lost my biological parents and my grandparents, who had adopted me. I had battled infertility and lost my father-in-law. But this time, the grief was heavier, and instead of sadness, I felt anger.

I wished someone had said, "I can't imagine how hard this must be for you," or even simply, "I'm so sorry." I wanted, and deserved, acknowledgement for the weight I was carrying. Ultimately, I wanted to feel seen.

I had always projected a version of me that had it all together, fooling everyone, especially myself. Through all the losses, I planned funerals, wrote obituaries, and cleaned out homes. I wrote thank-you notes and made the necessary arrangements. Behind my smile, my stomach was always in knots, and my heart raced constantly. Sudden and unexplained panic attacks left me breathless, my chest tight, my mind racing. This was all new; I had never experienced panic attacks or this kind of unrelenting anxiety before. Every racing heartbeat was a warning that something inside me was unraveling.

REDEFINING SELF

One of the hardest parts of a script break is losing a clear sense of who you are. The roles and identities that once made sense no longer feel true. It's hard enough to manage disruption, but even harder to ask questions: Who am I now? What's next?

I don't remember a time in my life when I wasn't taking care of someone else. Being dependable wasn't just something I did; it was who I was. When my mother-in-law was diagnosed with Stage IV lung cancer, I dove in without hesitation. Right away, she moved in with my husband, son, and me, and suddenly, we had constant chemotherapy, immunotherapy, pulmonology, oncology, and general practice appointments. We had home visits three times a week from a home health nurse, physical therapist, and occupational therapist, and I had a color-coordinated calendar, a to-do list that was ten miles long, and a smile.

> *I had a color-coordinated calendar, a to-do list that was ten miles long, and a smile.*

I typed emails in the oncology waiting room, hid in the hospital bathroom to take work calls, and sat with Jan while she napped, updating my calendar.

I never missed one of my son's home games, and I packed snacks for the team. I helped him study for exams in between tasks and planned sleepovers and parties. I prioritized my husband, his health, and his career.

I had taken care of my parents as they aged. I focused on making their lives easier, from taking them grocery shopping to appointments, to painting sheds and fences, and having renovations done on their home to make it more accessible. I drove the three and a half hours home at least one weekend a month, using that time to help them clean and do other necessary chores. After all, they had put their life on hold to raise me when they adopted me in their late forties; it was the least I could do for them.

In my career, I have always worked in an assistant-type role. Anticipating needs and taking care of others came naturally to me, and I excelled at it, but it also conditioned me to ignore my own needs. I managed schedules, calendars, and appointments, and anticipated meeting needs such as agendas, minutes, and follow-ups.

I also took care of my beloved husband after two hip replacements, a knee replacement, arthroscopic surgery, and back surgeries, along with countless procedures. He has a disability called Multiple Epiphyseal Dysplasia, which he was born with, and sometimes uses a wheelchair. He has trouble standing for longer than half an hour, and I am always looking for ways to make his life easier.

Anytime someone said, "I don't know how you are doing it all," I felt pride surge through me. I was "doing it all," and I was doing it well! It was a badge of honor. I worked from every appointment, every waiting room, somehow managing to keep all the balls in the air.

Or so I thought.

When It All Shattered

My script break was a slow buildup that was years in the making. Jan's death was the final straw. Suddenly, how I had dealt with previous losses wasn't working, and I had to make changes. It wasn't just about losing Jan; it was about losing the version of me who had been holding it together for so long. The version of me that was always on top of things, well put together, and never missing a beat.

The silence from work was also shattering, and it made me realize that the world had moved on, but I couldn't.

We are taught to smile through the pain and show up for work and obligations as if nothing has happened. Real strength isn't pretending you are fine. Real strength is admitting when your script has broken and having the courage to rebuild something new.

CULTURAL EXPECTATIONS

Acknowledging that your script is broken isn't easy. We are taught to be strong and push through script breaks, getting back to "normal" as soon as possible (after all, you get three days of bereavement leave!).

No one tells you that your normal may no longer exist. You're not just trying to get back on your feet — you are standing in the rubble of the life, dreams, and expectations you once knew, expected to keep going as if nothing has changed. I know, because I did it.

Before the age of 44, I had lost my biological parents, my grandparents who adopted and raised me, married a man with a progressive disability, battled infertility, and lost my in-laws. I could teach a master class on deflection and pretending nothing had changed. Powdering my nose in the office bathroom after sobbing, then walking out with

I could teach a master class on deflection and pretending nothing had changed.

a smile on my face. Sitting through meetings dripping with sweat because of my fertility medications, but continuing the facade that everything was fine. It was early in my marriage, and I didn't want my husband to think I was weak. I was also building my career and wanted to prove I could handle it all while never missing a deadline.

I had been living two lives for a long time. One side of me was living in pain, feeling increasingly lost, isolated, overwhelmed, and drowning in grief. The other side was projecting the "ideal" me, prepared with deadlines and to-do lists, and earning rave performance reviews.

It wasn't until I acknowledged both sides that I could start to heal. Every heartbreak, disappointment, and shattered plan leaves behind a truth you couldn't have learned any other way. What broke you open can teach you how to rebuild stronger, clearer, and truer than before.

> *Every heartbreak, disappointment, and shattered plan leaves behind a truth you couldn't have learned any other way.*

PAUSE AND REFLECT

To preserve myself, I hit reset. I took a long, hard look at my life and was finally honest with myself about what was working and what wasn't. This wasn't about being vulnerable. It was survival. I knew something had to change, and I had to move from chaos to clarity.

During this process, I asked myself big questions I had never taken the time to consider. They centered on my values and how I wanted to live them. Everything had changed, and I had to decide how I wanted to live my life. Here are a few questions to consider:

- What is important to me?
- What do I value on a daily, monthly, and yearly basis?
- What did I value before?
- How have my values changed?
- How does this change impact how I live my life?

I sat down with a notebook and wrote down everything that mattered to me, and what didn't. I kept the notebook close for several days, jotting things down as they came to mind. I realized that some of my priorities, including achievement and being "the strong one," weren't what mattered most.

When I evaluated my list, I realized I was putting too much value on being dependable, busy, taking care of others, and accepting praise for holding it all together.

After the disruption and intense self-reflection, I realized my priorities had shifted. I wanted to live a life where I could make an impact, have a focused purpose, live with more freedom, and find ways to inspire others. The beauty of these choices is that they were already familiar. They were things I'd always loved and enjoyed, and now, I was fully embracing them.

THE MOMENTUM METHOD

Change starts with questions, and that's where the Momentum Method comes in. It wasn't born in a conference room on a whiteboard or created from scientific research. It was born out of necessity.

What had worked for me simply wasn't working anymore. The ways I had been coping, pushing through, and managing no longer allowed me to move forward. I was unraveling.

The path toward a new me wasn't planned out, but later I realized it followed phases. Each step built on the previous one and helped move me forward. When I came out on the other side, I realized how this approach could help others. That was the beginning of the Momentum Method.

My rebuilding momentum started when I took the first step and hit reset, allowing myself to grieve instead of rushing past it. I learned to give myself space and time to pause and steady myself. I found ways to calm the chaos in my mind in different ways, like taking walks when I felt panic rising.

The second step started when I named my struggles and allowed myself to admit I was sinking, sad, and unraveling. Giving a voice to my disruption was freeing.

Shifting past these struggles led me to the third step, where I allowed myself to dream on purpose, imagining a life that looked different than before. I dreamed of big, wild, audacious goals that had always been in the back of my mind.

Once those dreams took root, I began the fourth step and started rewriting my script and taking action. In July 2025, I quit my full-time position to do two things: start my own business and join my friend Dana at her consulting firm. It's been an incredible journey of self-exploration, patience, and momentum. That is where the Momentum Method was born, and that choice is what led me to write this book.

You may not be ready to quit your job or start a business, but you are ready to take the next step. You're not starting over. You're rebuilding forward, piece by piece, into a life that reflects who you are now.

You don't have to bounce back. You can't. You're not the same person anymore. It's time to rebuild forward.

REFLECTION:

What Do You Truly Want?

For our first reflection, I suggest you find a quiet place and something to write with (notebook, pen, etc.). We'll start with some big questions I realized I needed to think about but had never taken the time to consider.

After a break, everything is changed, and you get to choose how you want to live your life. The questions below center on your values at this moment in time. Think about how you might live those values in your everyday life.

Here are a few questions to consider:

- What is important to me?
- What do I value on a daily, monthly, and yearly basis?
- What did I value before?
- How have my values changed?
- How does this change impact how I live my life?

CHAPTER 2

Not Starting Over, Rebuilding Forward

When life breaks your script, it's only natural to try to go back to a familiar version of yourself. The challenge is that this version no longer exists. After my script break, I believed resilience meant getting back to normal as soon as possible. I tried to outwork the pain to prove that I was okay but was left spinning without any direction. Let's look at why this approach fails, how hustle culture feeds into the illusion, and what it means to rebuild forward.

BOUNCING BACK

We cling to the idea of bouncing back because it fools us into believing life can stay neat and predictable. Unfortunately, script breaks don't play by the rules.

When you face a script break in your life, people are quick to encourage you to bounce back as if you can dust yourself off and be the same person you were before. We are taught to grieve quietly and quickly, then get back to having it all together.

I used to believe that if I worked hard enough, I could return to who I was before everything broke. In the end, I learned there is no going back, only forward. The Momentum Method was born from that realization.

I remember the first day back at work after my mom died. I got up, dressed, did my hair and makeup, and drove to work. I greeted everyone with a smile as I walked in and filled my coffee. I made small talk and chatted. Then, I went to my office, closed the door, and sat on the floor, sobbing. I usually called her every morning on the way to work. That day, I drove in silence. The absence of her voice was deafening. I missed her so much my chest ached, as if the air was too heavy.

I only allowed myself a few minutes to fall apart because there was a meeting on my calendar. I wiped my tears and walked back out into the world like my life hadn't just shattered. I attended the meeting, offered suggestions, and volunteered for tasks, trying to prove that I was doing okay. I wasn't. I was hustling.

HUSTLE CULTURE

Hustle culture teaches us to avoid discomfort by staying busy. It pushes grief, feelings, and healing to the background, while getting back to business as usual is seen as strength. But all of this momentum doesn't move you forward. It avoids what keeps you in pain and needs attention.

Most workplaces offer you three days of bereavement leave. Three days to handle the worst days of your life. Three days to write an obituary, plan a funeral, bury your loved one, return all the casserole dishes, and somehow be back to normal.

Not long ago, I was at a conference and met up with a former colleague. I knew she had just lost her father, so I asked how she was. She quietly shared the weight of her grief — the emptiness and disorienting adjustments. She told me about the emotional toll, her difficulty concentrating, and how hard it is to balance work with managing someone's affairs. Then she looked at me and said, "I don't know how you've done it. You've had so much loss. How do you get through each day?" I wanted to say, "I cry in my car before work. I forget things, and I'm breaking." But instead, I smiled and gave her the line I had rehearsed a hundred times, "You do what you have to do." Even as I said it, I felt a pit in my stomach. Looking back, that would have been an incredible moment to honestly convey my feelings and struggles.

In both of those moments, I wasn't thriving. I wasn't even healing. I was hustling. I was doing what our culture rewards: pushing through, keeping up appearances, never missing a beat. The lie is that if you move fast enough and fill every hour, you'll bury the grief. But hustle doesn't heal. It hides.

Hustle doesn't heal. It hides.

The Busy Badge

Being busy is a defining characteristic of hustle culture, and I embraced it as part of who I was. It made me proud to be thought of as dependable, always saying "yes" when asked to come in early, stay late, or volunteer for another committee. When someone asked how things were, I would always respond with how busy things were. It felt like the fuller the calendar, the more it proves success.

Society tells us that if we move fast enough, plaster on a smile, and keep our schedules full, we can outrun our pain.

We are encouraged and celebrated for pushing harder, doing more, and being busy. Busyness is a badge everyone wants to earn and wear proudly. Often, when you ask someone how they are, they want to tell you how busy they are. They talk about how many activities their children are in, how many hours they work, and how stressed they feel. I am guilty of the same responses: how much I was doing, how many people depended on me. Their nods felt like validation.

Busyness is a fragile badge. It doesn't protect you; it disguises you. Behind the productivity, I was exhausted. I was unraveling. I was lonely.

> *Busyness is a fragile badge. It doesn't protect you; it disguises you.*

Maybe you've nodded through a meeting, barely hearing a word because your mind was somewhere else. Maybe you've volunteered for something you didn't have time for, just to prove you could handle it. Maybe you've forced a smile at the grocery store when all you wanted to do was cry.

Maybe you've answered, "I'm fine, just busy," when you weren't fine at all. Maybe you've scrolled social media, comparing your behind-the-scenes mess to someone else's curated highlight reel, and wondered why you couldn't keep up.

The world convinces you that if you keep moving, no one will notice you are falling apart.

Hustle Culture Is a Lie

Everywhere we look, hustle culture preaches *more*. Social media feeds are full of shiny quotes telling us to work harder. Influencers often use phrases like #Grind, #Slay, and #RiseAndGrind. Success is often measured by how many hours you are on the clock and how well you can pretend you're not exhausted.

Hustle culture doesn't just keep us busy. It takes things from us. The cost shows up in our bodies, in our relationships, and even in who we believe we are.

Stress wreaks havoc on your body, from sleepless nights to headaches to aching muscles. We convince ourselves these symptoms are normal, but our bodies are trying to tell us that it's too much. We need to slow down, and we are doing more than it can carry. I can't begin to recount all the sleepless nights I've had because my mind was racing and I was going through my endless to-do list. Often, I would just get up and work for a few hours until exhaustion took over.

Hustle also strains our relationships, from snapping at those we love to being unable to be fully present because we can't get away from the constant stream of emails and deadlines. Before you know it, you've missed the important events, birthdays, and celebrations. You may have been physically there, but you weren't truly present. Unfortunately, sometimes saying "yes" to someone else meant saying "no" to my family.

When I subscribed to hustle culture, many things fell through the cracks. I was breaking out in hives all over my body for months straight. I scheduled an appointment with an allergist who took several months to see. On the day of the appointment, I was busy at work and completely forgot the appointment. I was embarrassed and frustrated with myself. The very appointment that I needed the most was pushed aside because of the hustle. I was breaking out in hives from stress, and the stress made me miss the one appointment that could have helped. Instead of realizing the issue, I told myself that I should have done a better job managing my calendar, and I wouldn't let it happen again. That day, the badge of being busy didn't make me dependable; it cost me my health.

Another time, my son came home from school and was telling me about his day. I was sitting at my desk when I thought about an email that I needed to send. As he spoke, I turned to my computer and typed the email. Suddenly, he asked me a question, and I had no idea what he was talking about. I hadn't heard him because I was too focused on work. He was frustrated with me and stormed off. I had let work distract me from my top priority, my son.

The most significant cost is the belief that our worth is directly tied to output. We are so deeply embedded in hustle that we forget to ask ourselves what we want and what excites us. When I took a step back, I realized it had been years since I had thought about what I wanted.

Hustle culture will continue to demand more of you long after you've run out of energy to give. Eventually, I realized the old way — hustling, hiding, and pretending I was fine — was just survival on borrowed time.

A NEW APPROACH

What if we hustled in a different way, one rooted in honesty and self-compassion? What if we only hustled toward what actually mattered to us, focusing not on what mattered before or what looks good to others or even what others expect of us? That kind of hustle makes sense. With this approach, you hustle toward what lights you up, what you are excited to get out of bed for.

Hustle toward what lights you up.

Hopefully, you recognize now that hustling to recreate the life you had before everything changed will only keep breaking you. The new way to hustle focuses on rebuilding and working toward a life that fits where you are now.

No one plans for disruption. We plan for success, growth, vacations, milestones, and celebrations. We don't plan for the day the script breaks — when a marriage ends, a parent or child dies, when the doctor says it's cancer, or when the job disappears unexpectedly.

Rebuilding

Rebuilding doesn't happen until you are ready. Then, you'll begin hearing a quiet voice inside reminding you that, "You can't live like this." At first, it's muted. You can almost ignore it. But whispers don't go away. It will build until it becomes a steady drumbeat that overwhelms your mind, and you can no longer ignore it.

It's okay to listen and dream. You can't go back to the person you were, but you get to become someone new, someone stronger, someone rebuilding forward. Rebuilding isn't just something you read about; it's something you *learn and practice.*

REFLECTION:

Your Script Break

Think about a time when your story didn't go according to plan. Maybe it was a dream that didn't pan out, an unexpected betrayal or loss, or an identity shift you didn't expect. Take a few moments to reflect and then start writing. I've added a few questions to help you think about your break.

- Write out what happened and your emotions at that time.
- What changed?
- What message did you feel (or hear) from others about how you "should" handle it?
- Looking back, what do you feel that you've lost?

You don't have to have all the answers yet. You're learning to understand script breaks as both painful and hopeful.

CHAPTER 3

Living in the Aftermath

When life breaks your script, grief is always part of the "after." Script breaks force endings we didn't want, realities we didn't choose, and versions of ourselves we never expected to become. The truth is that grief rarely looks like we were taught it would. Sometimes it's quiet, subtle, and deeply internal.

THE MANY FACES OF GRIEF

It's important to understand the many faces and types of grief because even if you don't recognize or name it, the grief still changes you.

Whether it is a job you never got or a loss you saw coming a mile away, acknowledging and naming the script break gives it shape. It doesn't mean you have to solve it today, or even tomorrow, but it gives you something you can hold, examine, and rebuild from. In that moment of honesty, you reclaim your life and take control of what happens next.

There are many different faces of grief, and often it arrives unseen. It can start as a quiet sense that something is off — a vague heaviness, like carrying a backpack of bricks no one else can see. It digs into your shoulders, making you ache. Even though it hurts, you pretend you're okay.

Some losses are obvious, such as death, divorce, or losing a job. Others go unnamed, but they carry the same weight. We're taught that certain griefs are unacceptable, even trivial. Still, your heart isn't fooled.

There are many examples of grief we don't name. The different forms of grief that follow are some of the most common unacknowledged types of grief.

Loss of Self

Script breaks often trigger identity grief and loss of self. When the role you've held or the title you've worn changes, the grief runs much deeper than most realize.

Sometimes, a role you once cherished (spouse, parent, work title) becomes the only way people see you. When that role changes or disappears, you are left wondering, "Who am I now?"

I felt this way when I went through unsuccessful fertility treatments. The script I had written included me being a mother, and when that didn't happen, I grieved the identity that I had planned my life around. I celebrated friends who were having babies, planned their baby showers, and hid my disappointment. If anyone asked me about having children, I smiled and responded vaguely, saying it would happen soon. I didn't want anyone to know I was struggling.

Appointment after appointment, I allowed myself to hope, but I was met with disappointment. Internally, I felt broken. Externally, I acted as if I was taking it in stride, and the loss wasn't bothering me. I focused on my career and hobbies and worked to prove that I was "fine."

I grieved a lost sense of identity when I left Franklin College. For ten years, the college wasn't just where I worked; it was part of who I was. I attended sporting events and plays, and I mentored students I still keep in touch with today. People knew me as "Andrea from Franklin College," a title that made me feel like I belonged to something bigger than myself.

When it came time to leave, I knew it was the right decision for my professional growth. Walking off campus that last day felt like leaving a piece of myself behind. Packing up my office, handing in my keys, and saying goodbye to my colleagues, who had become family, was heartbreaking. Although I was excited for what was next, I was gutted by the loss of a community and identity I had cherished for a decade.

Afterward, when people asked what I did, I stumbled over my words. Without Franklin, who was I? It was a reminder that identity grief doesn't just come from relationships; it also comes from our roles, communities, and titles.

There is also grief when roles or expectations that are important and meaningful to you no longer fit. Maybe you're the dependable one who always organizes parties, events, and vacations, but you are exhausted. Perhaps you are in a position where you are excelling, but the "star employee" script no longer lights you up.

We don't owe anyone an explanation when we decide a role or expectation no longer fits, even if it will disappoint people who expect us to stay the same. Letting go isn't easy, but it's the only way to rebuild.

Loss of Belonging

Some of the deepest forms of grief come from losing a sense of belonging — losing connection to people or community. When the places, groups, or relationships you are in begin to change or disappear, you grieve the loss because there is comfort in being a part of something.

My husband, Justin, lost a community when he graduated from Indiana University with his Ph.D. in Mathematics. During those years, his cohort became family. They shared one giant office and had countless late-night study sessions fueled by pizza and wings. Weekends were spent together, and they pulled each other through brutal classes and demanding professors.

Then, it ended. Diplomas in hand, everyone scattered to jobs around the world. Bloomington had been a temporary stop in their lives, and suddenly, the community Justin loved was gone. Although they keep in touch on social media, it will never be the same.

This loss of belonging is often unnamed, but it is a very real form of grief.

Loss of Connection

Loss of connection can result from a variety of situations, including separation, estrangement, societal changes, division, or even the loss of a pet. You grieve because you feel separated from people, emotions, and your goals.

When my husband and I were undergoing fertility treatments, we decided to get a dog that we named Phoebe. I remember when we saw her at the pet store; she was in a crate with puppies of all different breeds. We asked if we could see her, and as soon as they opened the crate, all the puppies ran out! It was chaos. When we looked in the crate, she was still there, sitting in the back, the only one who hadn't run out. We instantly fell in love.

Phoebe was a salt-and-pepper miniature schnauzer with the most beautiful, silky coat. Instead of walking, she pranced with high, energetic steps that conveyed joy. Shortly after bringing her home, she developed kennel cough, then pneumonia and a collapsed lung.

She spent a week in a veterinary hospital but made a full recovery. When she came home, she became the center of our world. We adored her. We took her on trips, both in cars and on planes.

She was our constant companion. She followed me from room to room and slept in bed with us, her snore lulling me to sleep.

She comforted me after every failed fertility treatment, curling up beside me. She knew my emotions before I said a word. She carried me through the hardest seasons, the grief of losing parents, and she was there for the moments that changed our family for the better, like adopting our son when he was twelve. The two of them formed a bond instantly and adored each other.

The connection our family had with Phoebe was as strong as many human relationships. When it was time for her to cross the rainbow bridge, we were devastated. There are no words to describe it. I sat and held her paw as she passed, and I thanked her for always being there. I grieved in a way I didn't know was possible. The house felt unbearably empty without her little paws prancing across the floor.

Not everyone understands the loss of a pet. Often, we minimize our feelings to avoid being judged. Phoebe wasn't just a dog; she was the very definition of unconditional love, and she is irreplaceable. In losing her, I lost a piece of my heart, and I grieved that loss.

Loss of Safety

Disruption doesn't just break our routines; it often affects our sense of safety. The things we work to control tightly, like financial stability, relationships, and even our own strength, suddenly feel uncertain and out of control when life breaks the script, which can lead to unnamed grief.

Financial Insecurity

For example, financial insecurity isn't only about numbers on a spreadsheet — it's also about the panic you feel from an unexpected car repair, the sinking feeling when the heating or air goes out, or staying up late to decide what you need to give up that month. Financial stress can lead to anxiety, depression, sleep problems, and can even affect your self-worth. This grief may be invisible to others, but it's debilitating to the person suffering.

Physical Effects

Safety isn't only about physical protection. You can also feel a loss of safety if it seems like your inner world might collapse.

Sometimes losing the feeling of safety shows up in your body. Over a period of several weeks, I became extremely worried about my health. My heart was racing, and I was having trouble breathing. I would gasp for air and feel as though I was breathing through a straw. It was awful, and I was terrified. Was I having a heart attack?

I made a doctor's appointment, but in the meantime, I had an appointment with my counselor. I told her about my symptoms and how worried I was that something was wrong with my lungs, and she began asking me questions about how often it happened and when it started. She listened carefully and then said, "You are having panic attacks."

I looked at her in disbelief. Panic attacks? That hadn't even crossed my mind. I thought there was something physically wrong with me.

The next week, I saw my doctor, and she confirmed that my lungs were clear and my heart was fine. I was shocked. It stunned me to realize my body had been carrying grief and stress so loudly that I felt like something was seriously wrong with me. Yet I had been ignoring it.

Past Abuse or Emotional Neglect

The absence of safety, love, or affirmation carries emotional scars and baggage. This results in a form of grief that we often keep hidden from others.

We adopted our nephew when he was twelve, but we had been trying to adopt him since he was born. Unfortunately, before he came to live with us, he didn't always live in a safe, loving, or affirming home. Although we love him unconditionally and provide him with a safe and loving home, he carries the scars of his past, and he grieves the childhood he wishes he'd had. Sometimes this grief surfaces in the form of self-doubt, mistrust, or feelings of abandonment. Sadly, no matter when in your life you face abuse or emotional neglect, it follows you into your relationships, your work, and the way you view yourself. It's a poignant reminder of how deeply neglect can shape our self-perception.

As parents, it's heartbreaking that we can't erase those early wounds. All we can do is love him and be there for him. We hope that with our support and his counselor's guidance, his emotional scars will fade over time.

Fear of Being a Burden

Worrying that you will be a burden to loved ones in the future can create unseen grief. This is something that bothers my husband, Justin. He was born with a rare disability called Multiple Epiphyseal Dysplasia and, as a result, has had twenty-three surgeries, including hip and knee replacements, multiple back surgeries, and laminectomies. At forty-six years old, doctors say he has the arthritis of someone in their eighties.

Through it all, he is the most positive man you will ever meet. He jokes with nurses before surgery, never complains when he is in pain, and refuses to let his disability define him. Every so often, his fear of being a burden when we're older creeps in.

It doesn't matter that I reassure him that I love him. and I'll be here with him for the long haul; the fear is always lingering in the background. We've had many late-night conversations about what our future might hold. It's a reminder that grief isn't only about what you've lost; sometimes it's about what we're afraid might be ahead.

None of us wants to be a burden to those we love, yet there are times when we have to be dependent on others. That's not weakness, it's strength.

Grieving Lost Possibilities

Sometimes disruption and grief don't come from something that happened; they can also come from what never did, like the dreams that slipped through our fingers or the possibilities of the path not taken.

Lost Opportunities

Sometimes grief shows up in what we see as the road not taken. You think about the "what ifs" — the college you didn't attend, the job you didn't take, the relationship you didn't pursue. These losses are rarely discussed but are very real and painful. When the door you didn't open is closed for good, it can feel like regret, emptiness, envy, and grief.

Loss of the Life We Imagined

We have all created a script for how our life was supposed to go. When it detours or unravels, it can feel like a death. The grief is real. You are mourning the version of you who was supposed to be living that life.

A LOST DREAM

In 2021, I left Franklin College, where I had been for ten years, to follow a dream: working at Salesforce. For me, Salesforce wasn't just a job — it represented a culture I admired, a salary that would ease financial stress, incredible benefits, and work that would energize and excite me.

I applied for sixteen positions and interviewed for nine, making it to the final round for several. I made connections with twenty-seven Salesforce employees, working LinkedIn like it was my full-time job. I met amazing people who connected me with hiring managers, colleagues, and human resources. I created a cheat sheet for every position and every person I met. I wrote two blog posts on LinkedIn about why Salesforce should hire me, reaching hundreds of people.

It was a dream I was going to make come true, fueled by ambition and sheer willpower. I told everyone about it who would listen, taking pride in the risks I was taking and the persistence I was showing. I was sure it would pay off.

I prepared for each interview as if I were being interviewed by the FBI. I researched every position meticulously, practiced questions and responses, and recorded myself giving presentations so I could critique every word and gesture. Many late nights were spent hunched over my laptop, rehearsing answers. When the final rounds came, I poured my heart into them, working day and night.

Every email I received set off a jolt of adrenaline: Was this finally the one?

Month after month, coffee after coffee, and interview after interview, I hadn't gotten any offers. With every unanswered email and long pause after an interview, I began to grieve a dream I could feel slipping away.

> I didn't get the job. I replayed each interview in my head. What did I do wrong? Was I too eager? Was I not enough?
>
> I was devastated. Embarrassed. I felt like a failure. After all the interviews, all the networking, all the hours of preparation, I was left with nothing.
>
> When I got the email that I wasn't selected for the final position, I sat at my computer, numb. The tears came all at once, and I allowed myself to break down, at home, where no one could see me. Looking back, I realize it wasn't just about losing the job; I had lost a version of myself that I believed in. But I grieved silently, believing it wasn't "big enough" to count.

ANTICIPATORY GRIEF

Anticipatory grief creeps in before the goodbye. The knot in your stomach tightens long before the door actually closes.

Some reasons for anticipatory grief might include:

- Terminal diagnosis
- Chronic illness
- Impending divorce
- The slow loss of a loved one through dementia
- A beloved pet nearing the end
- Aging parents

Anticipatory grief is strong and overwhelming; you feel it in your gut long before it's "time." It also includes mourning a future you know is slipping away.

My parents (biological grandparents) began preparing me for their deaths when I was very young. This might sound strange, or even harsh, but it was the reality of our situation. If they showed me how to do something and I asked how to do it again, they would say, "What would you do if we weren't here?" I didn't realize it at the time, but this created an awareness that loss could come at any moment. This stuck with me, and it was only when writing this book that I realized what a big part anticipatory grief has played in my life.

I never attended preschool or summer camps, so when I started kindergarten, it was the first time I had ever been away from home. It was also my first experience with anxiety. When I got on the bus to head to kindergarten, I was homesick in a way that felt physical. I would ask to go to the restroom, but instead, I would sneak down to the front office. There was a phone hanging on the teacher's wooden mail slots, and Mom had taught me our phone number. I would pull over a chair, climb up, and call Mom, holding the cold metal receiver against my cheek. Relief washed over me the moment I heard her voice on the other end.

She always answered. She would ask me how my day was going and then tell me to go back to class. I would hang up, climb down, and walk back to the classroom like nothing had happened.

I did this for a few months before I was caught.

This continued into adulthood, with the fear worsening. The phone calls just changed from the school office to my cell phone. I called home multiple times a day to check in. I carried a deep fear that something would happen and I wouldn't be there. If I couldn't reach them, I would spiral into a panic. My throat would tighten, my thoughts would race, and my heart rate would skyrocket. The fear was the same; it had simply grown up with me.

This is anticipatory grief. The idea of losing my parents early in my life was breaking the idyllic script I had created for my life.

Anticipatory grief is the pit in your stomach before layoffs or restructuring are announced. It's the uneasy silence in meetings. Recognizing this type of grief enables us to support one another and create workplaces where people feel seen, even before the loss occurs. For me, that fear of loss was always a shadow, teaching me that good moments carried the possibility of goodbye.

YOU'RE NOT ALONE

If you recognize yourself in one or several of these scenarios, you are not alone. These are real losses, and your heart doesn't measure grief by how (or if) others see it.

When a loss isn't publicly acknowledged or validated, it is called disenfranchised grief. This can include the loss of a friendship or a dream job that didn't happen. We feel we need to hide this type of grief because it doesn't fit society's script for "real loss."

This disenfranchised type of grief is excruciating because it isolates you. You may feel as though you don't have "permission" to grieve — or that if you did share, no one would understand. It doesn't just silence your grief; it silences you.

From Grief to Starting Point

Grief may begin as a quiet heaviness or an ache, but naming it is an act of courage. Whether your loss is visible or carried in silence, giving it shape allows you to set it down, even for a moment. When you name the grief, whatever form it takes, you begin to loosen its grip. That's where momentum starts — not in bouncing back, but in choosing to rebuild forward.

> *Grief may begin as a quiet heaviness or an ache, but naming it is an act of courage.*

THE MOMENTUM METHOD

Grief doesn't stop because we recognize it, but it is the first step. There's no quick fix to the grief you've suffered. But there is a way to move through grief instead of being buried by it. You don't need a ten-step life overhaul; you just need movement to get unstuck. That's where the Momentum Method comes in.

The Momentum Method isn't just a framework; it's the process I lived through that allowed me to rebuild my life. Loss, layered with caretaking, burnout, identity shifts, and pressure, led me to it. That moment on Jan's floor, sobbing as I cleaned out her kitchen, made me realize the old way wasn't working. I couldn't keep pretending. I had to get honest and messy.

The Momentum Method isn't about bouncing back; it's about rebuilding forward. Each step gives you momentum for the next, helping you breathe, name what's been lost, reconnect with yourself, dream again, and take real steps toward a future you are excited about. I wasn't looking for a grand "life overhaul." In fact, that would have seemed too overwhelming. But small, practical steps, stacked gently, gave me momentum to take the next one.

These steps won't fix the pain from your script break, but they will give you a rail to hold when everything feels slippery. They will help you when you've accidentally stepped on black ice, and you feel as though your feet are sliding out from under you. Grab hold of these steps for the support you need.

The Steps

I know what you are carrying. Here are the steps and a brief explanation of how and why they might help.

Step 1: Hit Reset – Pause and create space to breathe.

Sometimes the bravest thing you can do is pause, quiet the chaos, and find your footing. Grief doesn't care about your deadlines, meetings, or the fact that you were just trying to get groceries without crying. When it hits, it hits. Hitting reset quiets the chaos long enough for you to catch your breath.

Step 2: Call It What It Is – Name your loss honestly.

In order to stop pretending and start moving forward, it's important to name your loss honestly. Whether it's the death of a loved one, the dream you never got to live, or the life you thought you'd have, you are allowed to be angry about it; you can shout and scream about it. If it makes you feel better to cuss and stomp, then do it. Don't downplay or disguise your feelings. Calling it like it is breaks its power.

Step 3: Get Back to You – Reconnect with values and boundaries.

Assess, evaluate, and realign your values. Set boundaries and rediscover the version of you that's been hiding. Reconnect with what matters to you. I realized my job as an assistant, while a good job, no longer fulfilled me. I had been in survival mode for so long, I hadn't thought about what excited me or what I really wanted to do.

Step 4: Dream on Purpose – Give yourself permission to imagine.

When I allowed myself to dream on purpose, I started brainstorming to create a plan about how I wanted my life and career to look, complete with pros and cons, and how the plan worked with my values. Wanting more isn't selfish.

Give yourself permission to imagine a future that excites you again, even when today feels heavy. Dreaming isn't an indulgence; it's fuel.

> *Dreaming isn't an indulgence; it's fuel.*

Step 5: Rewrite Your Script – Turn your hopes into action.

Rebuilding forward is about authorship; you get to hold the pen and write your own story. When I left my full-time job in July 2025, I was rewriting my script. The old way wasn't working, and I owed it to myself to take a chance and do work that excites me.

I know that grief and disruption make everything harder, from decision-making, routines, and sometimes, getting out of bed.

You might feel too tired to follow a five-step plan because you are just trying to get through one day at a time. That's okay, this isn't about rushing. Momentum isn't about speed; it's about direction. You will realize the road ahead may not look like the one you imagined, but it can still be rich with meaning, growth, and possibility. It's okay if you can only take one small step right now.

> *Momentum isn't about speed; it's about direction.*

The Momentum Method isn't linear. Some days you will move forward, some days you will slide back. Progress isn't erased by hard days. Think of it like waves; sometimes you are carried forward effortlessly, and sometimes you are pulled back — but you keep moving. In the next section, I'll discuss each of these steps along with practical tools and strategies to help you implement them.

PART 2

THE MOMENTUM METHOD

CHAPTER 4

Step 1 – Hit Reset

Let's begin our rebuilding journey by hitting reset. This step is about pausing, quieting the noise, and giving yourself permission to rest.

I remember sitting in a meeting at work, pen in hand, nodding at the right times and updating my to-do list as if I were fully present. Inside, my heart was racing, and my chest was tight. I was one deep breath away from breaking down. Still, I continued to smile, write, and pretend I was fine. The fear of judgment from colleagues stopped me from getting up. On the outside, I looked composed, capable, and even confident. I was fooling everyone, including myself.

RECOGNIZING YOU ARE IN A SPIRAL

The hardest part of a spiral is knowing when you're in one; sometimes it sneaks up quietly, and before you know it, you are spinning in the middle of it.

Grief, stress, and disruption don't always look like you are falling apart. Sometimes chaos looks like over-functioning, micromanaging, people-pleasing, or emotional numbing. All of these are common, but they bury the grief you need to name before you can hit reset and start to move forward.

▶ **Over-functioning.** Convincing yourself that you can do more. After all, if you stay busy enough, you don't have time to acknowledge what's happening.

While clearing out Jan's house in the evenings after work and on the weekends, I also cleaned and organized every closet in my own house. Organizing made me feel calm when I was drowning. At Jan's, the house was in disarray, with boxes everywhere. Items were being set aside for Goodwill, trash, sale, and the dreaded "go through later" stack. I couldn't stand to come home to additional disorganization. I would stare at anything in my house that felt out of place until I fixed it, even if I was exhausted.

There are hidden costs to over-functioning: a short fuse, resentment, and moments when you snap at the ones you love most. I felt angry with myself for not being able to handle more. Everywhere I looked, other working moms were juggling it all with ease, and it seemed like they weren't just doing more, but doing it better. It never occurred to me that they were probably breaking in their own ways, too.

▶ **Micromanaging.** Clinging to control when things feel uncertain. It may appear as perfectionism, but it's a disguise.

STEP 1 – HIT RESET

Micromanaging made me feel in control during a time when everything was in chaos. With all that was going on, I was genuinely worried that if I didn't write down every step, I would forget. But I was also trying to control the chaos by micromanaging everything.

Lists became my lifeline. I'd give my husband and son detailed, itemized to-do lists, even for simple tasks. Grocery lists grew longer and more specific, down to the smallest detail, so nothing could be forgotten. Stacks of sticky notes cluttered my desk, kitchen counter, and even my car. But after a list or task was completed, I didn't feel relieved. I felt more anxious and frustrated with myself because what should have taken five minutes had taken an hour. Instead of easing my mind, the lists made me feel as if I was falling behind before I had even started.

▶ **People-pleasing.** Always saying yes and avoiding conflict, even if it leaves you exhausted and unfulfilled.

I volunteered for every extra task and committee at work, even while cleaning out Jan's house, managing her estate, and helping my husband and son through their grief. I didn't want to let anyone down.

▶ **Emotional numbing.** Doing anything you can to avoid what you are feeling.

I filled silence with noise, from podcasts to TV to scrolling on social media; I never sat in silence. In the quiet, I would have had to face my grief, so I stayed busy instead.

GOING THROUGH THE MOTIONS

By implementing the tactics above, we feel like we're showing the world that we have it all together — showing up to everything, meeting deadlines, and answering every email. We are physically present but emotionally detached.

I smiled on Zoom, gave updates in meetings, and consistently met deadlines with stellar performance reviews. I hid the fact that I wasn't sleeping and was having panic attacks. I didn't want anyone to see me fall apart. Instead of recognizing my spiral, I told myself things like, "Hold it together" and "You don't have time to fall apart."

Individually, these behaviors may appear harmless. After all, who doesn't want to be organized, helpful, and needed? It's when you string them together that you start to see your spiral. It's a silent unraveling that you hide from everyone, including yourself, because on the outside, you look like you are thriving.

A high-functioning spiral is still a spiral

You are showing up for everyone else, juggling all your responsibilities and excelling at them. Your busyness is a badge of honor, and you take pride in doing it all. When people ask you to add something to your overflowing plate, you take it as a compliment.

A high-functioning spiral is still a spiral

Aren't you exhausted?

You are white-knuckling your way through the day and trying not to explode. The danger is that you are performing so well that no one notices your slow unraveling. Eventually, even the most put-together spiral will collapse. Acknowledge your spiral without shame.

STEP 1 – HIT RESET

> **CHECK-IN: DEFINE YOUR SPIRAL**
>
> Grab your notebook and take a few moments to reflect. We've discussed over-functioning, people-pleasing, and emotional numbing. These are all real behaviors we use when we are in survival mode. They are signs that you are in a storm, even if no one else sees it.
>
> Think about these questions and jot down your thoughts:
>
> - What does your spiral look like? What are the things you do when you are overwhelmed, stressed, or avoiding difficult emotions?
> - Which behaviors did you see in yourself — or would you add your own? Do you check out emotionally or tell everyone that you're fine even when you're not?
> - What happens to you physically when you are in a spiral?
>   - Do you clench your jaw or get headaches?
>   - Does your heart race or feel like it's beating out of your chest?
>   - Do you get lightheaded?
>   - Do you feel like you can't breathe and are struggling to catch your breath?
>   - Do you feel like your mind is spiraling?
>
> Naming it doesn't fix it, but it gives it shape. When something has shape, you can face it and work with it. Most importantly, you can reset.

HITTING RESET

Sometimes the bravest thing you can do is reset. Hitting reset is about quieting the chaos, catching your breath, and finding your footing.

Simone Biles, 11-time Olympic medalist, famously hit reset during the Tokyo 2020 Games when she experienced the "twisties." The twisties are described as a "mental block that creates a dangerous disconnect between mind and body while gymnasts are airborne." It causes a gymnast to lose the sense of where their body is while in the air.

Simone's twisties were likely a result of intense mental stress and pressure. She said she was "fighting for her body and mind while trying to show up for her team. You've been doing something for so long, and now you no longer have control. It's terrifying."[1]

Sound familiar?

Simone hit reset by taking a break from gymnastics, withdrawing from the Olympic Games, attending therapy, and allowing herself to enjoy activities outside her sport. She chose safety, honesty, and rest over pushing through. She recognized her spiral and put herself first, an act of extraordinary courage under the world's brightest spotlight.

I remember watching Simone's story unfold in the media along with the criticism that followed. I was proud of her, not because of her athleticism, but because of her humanity. She mirrored what we were all feeling during the COVID-19 lockdown — the feeling of losing control in a world that demanded we keep going, despite our worries. The difference was that she did it under the world's spotlight, while I was hiding behind Zoom screens and endless to-do lists.

It took incredible courage for Simone to hit reset. She was judged, misunderstood, and accused of letting her team down. She knew the truth: pushing through wasn't brave, pausing was.

Ways to Hit Reset

Just because your spiral isn't visible to everyone does not mean it isn't happening. It's still a spiral. And while recognizing you are in a spiral is one thing, getting out of it is another.

Most of us can't take a vacation, time off work, or time away from our families just to rest. However, there are small things you can do every day to create moments of rest. Everyone deserves stillness.

Here are some things I prioritized when I realized I was in a spiral:

Rest. Even if it was only for 15 minutes, I'd lie on the bed in a quiet room, eyes closed, with my favorite blanket, and make myself rest. I wouldn't fall asleep, but it calmed me. Sometimes I'd put on my headphones, still at my desk, and listen to music without the distraction of email or Teams messages. These small pauses helped me to feel less overwhelmed.

Stop Multitasking. I am the self-proclaimed queen of multitasking. I can work, talk on the phone, and binge-watch a TV series simultaneously. I have a difficult time sitting down to watch a TV show or movie without doing something else at the same time. To quiet my mind and allow myself a reset, I forced myself to do one thing at a time. This allowed me to be completely present in what I was doing.

This is a practice that I will always struggle with. My best friend Andrea (yes, we have the same name) and I live about three hours apart, but we talk daily. I used to multitask during our calls, missing parts of the conversation because I was responding to an email or updating our family budget. Now, I sit down or take a walk while we talk with no chores or distractions. Our time together is precious, and I don't want to miss it because I need to fold laundry.

Find a creative outlet. Creativity became one of my resets. For me, it was oil painting, but for you, it might be something entirely different. The act of creating gives your mind permission to rest. You might write, bake, garden, build, decorate, play music, or doodle in a notebook. The point isn't the outcome; it's giving yourself space to create without judgment. It doesn't have to be perfect to be meaningful.

Your reset list will be different from mine, and you'll need to determine what works best for you and your situation. It may take trial and error to find the right fit, but the benefits are so worth it.

REFLECTION:

Your Permission Slip

Give yourself permission to pause, even if it's just long enough to take a breath. Acknowledge that you have faced a script break and you have been gritting your teeth for far too long.

Take a moment to reflect on what you truly need and write it down. The permission you give yourself can be big or small; it's not about rules or checklists, it's about grace. Sometimes it's serious, and sometimes it's just giving yourself permission to feel.

Here are some examples:

1. Today, I give myself permission to rest without guilt. The world won't fall apart if I take fifteen minutes to pause.
2. Today, I give myself permission to do something I enjoy, even if my to-do list isn't finished. Joy is just as important as the items on my list.
3. Today, I give myself permission to feel sad. I don't have to hide it, and I don't have to explain it to anyone.

Keep your list where you'll see it every day as a reminder and refer to it often. The list is just for you, and you don't have to share it with anyone.

Each item on the list is a reminder that you are allowed to make yourself a priority. Giving yourself permission is the first small reset that makes the bigger resets possible.

You've just completed Step One of the Momentum Method: Hit Reset. Every rebuild begins the moment you stop surviving and start choosing to breathe again.

CHAPTER 5

Step 2 – Call It What It Is

Society tells us to hide our grief, cover our dark circles, and plaster on a smile, no matter what is happening behind the scenes. We've been trained to keep moving, stay positive, and "look for the silver lining." After creating some peace in the chaos in the first step by hitting reset, you're ready for Step Two of the Momentum Method, which involves naming what you're feeling. You're allowed to be sad, angry, disappointed, and honest about every part of it.

Growing up, my family often talked about my biological parents, Mike and Lisa Masterson. They passed away in a motorcycle accident when I was just nine months old. Lisa died instantly, and Mike was supposed to recover. However, in the middle of the night at the hospital, a blood clot broke loose and went through his heart, killing him instantly.

I don't have a memory of the first time we talked about them; they were just woven into my childhood as part of my history, something I always knew. They were in love and had married at a young age. Lisa was beautiful and intelligent. She worked as a timekeeper in an automotive factory. Although Mike had grown up with a problematic family, Lisa's parents and brother had embraced him as their own, and he worked in the coal mines with my dad (maternal grandfather) and my brother (maternal uncle).

When they passed, there was an immediate custody battle between my maternal grandparents and my paternal grandmother. When my maternal grandparents (Mom and Dad) won, my paternal grandmother left the courtroom, and I never heard from or saw her again. I often wonder if she ever thinks of me. If she passed me on the street, would she recognize me? Would I recognize her?

MESSY TRUTH

Mom and Dad always talked about the positive aspects of my parents' death. They were grateful it was an accident, and there was no one to blame. Both of them had died suddenly without suffering, and they believed there was a reason for their deaths. I was taught to be grateful before I ever learned to be angry. In fact, I would feel guilty when I got angry and questioned why this tragedy had happened to our family.

Looking back, I was raised to overlook the messy truth and focus on the silver lining, a pattern that followed me into adulthood. My healing didn't start until I learned to look at the messy truths and name them.

We are conditioned to minimize pain, but this makes people feel guilty for looking at and thinking about their real, messy emotions.

We are conditioned to minimize pain, but this makes people

STEP 2 – CALL IT WHAT IT IS

feel guilty for looking at and thinking about their real, messy emotions. If you are grieving a job loss, it can feel humiliating. If you are going through a divorce, it can feel cruel. If you are undergoing grueling medical treatments, it can feel unfair. By not using words like "humiliating," "cruel," and "unfair," we aren't being truthful. It's like sealing our pain inside a beautifully wrapped box and pretending what's inside doesn't stink.

By naming your disruption, grief, or burnout and "calling it what it is," you're taking away its power and allowing yourself to feel and heal your emotions. When you don't look at or address those emotions, they don't go away; they fester.

It's time to drop the facade and call things what they really are.

AVOIDING THE TRUTH

The outside world is urging us to pick up the pieces and move on as quickly as possible, even when we're not ready.

From a young age, we are taught that difficult feelings make people uncomfortable. When you cry, someone hands you a tissue before you even finish your sentence. The unspoken rule is clear: Keep your emotions in check so they are easier for others to handle.

Avoidance isn't just a habit; it's a learned skill.

Keeping feelings hidden behind a mask of composure is especially expected at work, where it's an unspoken rule that emotions should be kept in check. Workplace culture has taught us that we don't discuss emotions related to burnout, job satisfaction, and team dynamics. When you mention burnout, you are often told, "Just power through." If you hint about job dissatisfaction, you are reminded to "Be grateful you have a job." Over time, we internalize these messages, and avoidance becomes a natural response.

> *Avoidance isn't just a habit; it's a learned skill.*

Avoidant Behaviors

Instead of facing a problem, it feels easier to avoid it, put it off, or simply ignore it. While such responses may, at first, provide short-term relief, they eventually make things worse. Avoidance habits take different forms, but here are a few common ones:

Avoiding people, places, and situations that remind you of your script break.

For three years, I avoided shopping in stores, opting instead to purchase everything online. Shopping had been one of my favorite things to do with my mom. We could find something to buy at any store. We would wander up and down every aisle, try things on, and laugh. Some of my favorite memories were at Walmart and JCPenney. After she passed away, the only store I could go into was the grocery store. Shopping in department stores brought back a flood of memories, reminding me of her and what I had lost. I avoided Walmart, Target, malls, boutiques, and even craft stores. Avoiding stores felt safer than dealing with the truth and the pain of her loss.

Convincing yourself and others that you are fine.

After Jan passed, my good friend Hannah arranged a pedicure at a salon for just the two of us. She brought snacks, wine, and we had the whole salon to ourselves. She went out of her way to make it special.

At one point, she asked me how I was doing. The truth was, I was unraveling. Instead, I forced a smile, took a sip of wine, and replied that I was fine, and changed the subject. I wish I had confided in her because she would have listened without judgment. Instead, pretending I was fine was easier, and saying out loud that I was falling apart would have made it too real.

Distracting yourself with activities that push away bad thoughts or feelings.

I have a friend who immersed herself in exercise after a major life disruption. What started as a healthy outlet quickly took over her life. She spent hours in the gym, skipping family dinners and turning down invitations from friends. On the surface, she looked strong and disciplined. Underneath, the workouts had become her armor; every mile and rep was a way to outrun pain she didn't want to face.

Avoidance allows us to give the appearance that we're fine. We can continue to play the perfect spouse, parent, employee, and friend. We fool ourselves into thinking the avoidance is for everyone else. We don't want to make them uncomfortable or be an inconvenience. You may be fooling your family, friends, and colleagues, but you aren't fooling yourself. You are wearing a mask, and eventually, it will crack.

IT'S OKAY TO FEEL BAD

Society encourages us to "Be positive!" and to "Look on the bright side." But you are allowed to be angry, disappointed, and grieving when things don't go the way you expected or wanted. A disruption isn't fair, and it's not what you had planned. That's the truth, and you deserve to feel it.

Consider this: When a friend approaches you about something awful and messy that's happened to them, what is your first instinct? Would you say, "At least you have…" or "It's all going to work out"? These responses show you mean well and want to make things better, but you move the conversation past their feelings toward an as-yet-unknown solution. What if, instead, you listened without rushing to point out the silver lining? That moment of sharing could give them space to feel their feelings within the safety of your friendship.

Most importantly, before you feel okay, it's okay to feel bad. You've just experienced a huge script break, and you don't have to feel up to feeling grateful or happy.

Sometimes the most healing thing for you to do is say, "I am not grateful for this. I didn't want this. I hate it, and it hurts." You don't have to censor yourself, and you don't have to coat it in gratitude to be socially acceptable.

My friend Emily taught me this lesson in the rawest way possible.

EMILY'S STORY

Four years ago, my friend Emily's world shattered when her brother, Andrew, died in a tragic accident. He was only forty-two years old and was married with three boys. The loss was devastating, and one of those moments that splits life into a clear *before* and *after*.

In those first days, a family member said through tears, "Something good will come from this." Emily remembers thinking, "Do you really think that?" She didn't want silver linings; she wanted her brother back. In those moments, there isn't comfort in meaning, only the unbearable fact that the person you love is gone.

Over time, Emily noticed that some people avoided her because they weren't sure what to say, while others tried to be encouraging, offering phrases like "He's in a better place," "That was his path," or the most used, "Everything happens for a reason." Although those words are meant to be comforting, they're often not what we need in those moments. What she wanted was honesty and someone to say the truth out loud: This is unbearable.

I checked in with her often, asking how she was doing and reminding her that she didn't have to sugarcoat her feelings. Some days, she would text about how exhausted she felt from holding it all together. When we spoke, I didn't try to fix her pain or search for the right words. I simply said, "Yes, it's unfair. I'm so sorry." I gave her the space to call it what it was — unfair, devastating, and life-altering. It reminded me how often we mistake comfort for compassion. Compassion isn't about soothing the pain; it's being willing to stand inside it with someone else.

Later, she told me how much it meant that I didn't try to fix her grief. She appreciated that I gave her space to feel exactly how she felt, without any guilt or forced gratitude.

CALLING IT WHAT IT IS

We rush to comfort when what grief often needs is company. We reach for silver linings when honesty is what's truly needed. We put grief on a clock: three months, six months, a year, because the truth is uncomfortable. Both Emily and I hate the phrase, "The first year is the worst. It will get better." The truth is, there is no *better*; there is only *after*.

Years later, Andrew's legacy is incredible. His company started *Habelfest*, a fundraiser that continues his love of BBQ competitions. This annual event has raised nearly half a million dollars for local causes. When someone recently said to her, "Look at all the people who have benefited from this; it's amazing," Emily agreed, but quietly added, "I'd still rather have him back."

Today, Emily doesn't hide from her emotions. If she needs to cry, she cries, no matter where she is or who's around. "We need to teach our kids it's okay to cry," she said, "It's okay to feel exactly what they feel. You don't have to be strong for anyone."

Grief doesn't need us to fix it or find the silver lining. It needs us to call it what it is: unfair, painful, exhausting, and heartbreaking. Sometimes the most loving thing isn't reassurance that it will be okay; it's "You are right, it's awful. I'm here."

Calling it like it is doesn't erase the pain; it honors it and allows healing to begin.

SMILE FOR THE CAMERA

While Emily's story unfolded quietly, others have chosen to tell their story on the public stage. While public figures are expected to smile for the camera and say the right thing, some break the mold, and in doing so, give the rest of us permission to speak the truth.

When Ann Curry was removed from her co-anchor position on *The Today Show* after just a year, she later said she felt like she had "failed," despite giving it her all.[2] Before her, Deborah Norville described being let go from the same show as a crushing blow to her confidence.[3]

After the death of Heath Ledger, Michelle Williams said she missed him in every role — father, partner, and actor — and that losing him was not what she had planned.[4]

When Sheryl Sandberg's husband died unexpectedly, she wrote about the overwhelming emptiness she felt. She was honest about wanting her old life back, about wishing for Option A, and about how painful it was to live in Option B. In her book, Option A is the life she had with Dave, the life she loved and wanted. Option B was everything that came after losing him, the version she never asked for, but had no choice but to live.[5]

These women spoke openly and honestly about their loss, unfiltered and unpretty. They gave voice to what so many of us have felt but didn't know we were allowed to say.

Actor Andrew Garfield echoed that truth when he spoke about losing his mother: "I hope this grief stays with me. It's the unexpressed love I didn't get to tell her."[6] He allowed the world to see the truth of his love and loss. In a culture that tells men to "man up" and hide their emotions, his words mattered. He reminded us that pain isn't gendered and love doesn't disappear when someone dies.

These moments remind us that when people with the biggest stages tell the truth, they give the rest of us permission to do the same.

LET GRATITUDE BE REAL

There is a place for gratitude, and we should practice it. Studies show that practicing gratitude, such as keeping a gratitude journal, can help alleviate anxiety and depression, making it a generally beneficial practice.

If we're not careful, though, gratitude can become a mask we wear. We're told to be thankful, even when our hearts are breaking, and sometimes the pressure to "find the bright side" keeps us from telling the truth about how we are feeling.

I'm not suggesting that you never find the silver lining or never share what you are grateful for. I am giving you permission not to fake it when you don't feel like it.

NAME THE MONSTER

You've calmed the storm, and you are ready to look it in the eye. It's time for truth-telling and naming what changed, without avoiding or minimizing the truth. We are turning on the light in a dark room and naming the monster.

It's time to face your disruption head-on. No more running, and no more hiding. Don't sugarcoat the loss or your feelings. We spend so much time pretending we're not upset and minimizing our experiences that we forget we have the right to *feel* them.

Whatever your disruption came from, whether it be job loss, divorce, loss of identity, or losing someone you love, you deserve to be angry. Give yourself permission to say it out loud and uncensored.

Say it in the privacy of your own home, in the car, in a whisper, or in a shout. You are reclaiming your voice and embracing the moment you stopped editing your truth to make it easier for others to hear.

Calling it like it is, naming the monster, is the second step toward reclaiming your identity and your power. You cannot rebuild if you are pretending it never happened.

REFLECTION:

Write It Out

Write exactly how you feel: how unfair it is, how much it hurts, what you are angry or heartbroken about. Let it be messy! You can write in sentences, bullet points, a rant, a list of grievances... just write it all down.

If you are struggling with what to write, here are some unfiltered examples:

- I am divorced, disappointed, and angry. I didn't ruin my marriage or give up. I held it together until there was nothing left to hold. I'm grieving something I fought for, and I deserve to say that out loud.
- This isn't the motherhood I pictured. I love my child, but I mourn the life I thought we would have. I'm tired of pretending it's all joy and gratitude. I am grieving the version of parenthood I imagined, and it doesn't make me a bad parent — it makes me an honest one.
- I lost my job because someone else made a decision behind closed doors. I gave them late nights, weekends, and missed vacations, and they had no loyalty. I was disposable. I am furious, and I deserve to grieve.
- I am exhausted from caregiving. I love the person I am caring for, but the constant appointments, sleepless nights, and watching them decline are breaking me. I grieve the person they were before this illness, and I miss my old life.
- I am furious that I am sick. I don't deserve this, and I am so tired of pretending I am fine. I am trying to survive, and it's exhausting to be "inspirational" for other people.

After you have written it all down, read it out loud. Read it to yourself in the mirror. Own it. Then, put it in an envelope and wait. When you are ready, you can burn it, rip it, or shred it; just let it go. By naming your pain, you can learn how to live without it. You don't have to carry it anymore.

> **You've just completed Step Two of the Momentum Method: Call It Like It Is. Every rebuild gains power when you stop minimizing your pain and name it, so you know what changed.**

CHAPTER 6

Step 3 – Get Back to You

Life's disruptions tempt us to romanticize what was. Whether it's a different time of life or a particular relationship, disruption has a way of making us look at the past through rose-colored glasses. In the middle of a script break, we often glamorize the life we had before, forgetting the struggles that came with it. We also might find ourselves wishing to "get back to normal," but what we are missing may have been a life built on burnout, pressure, or pretending.

Your goal isn't to return to normal after a disruption. You aren't the same person you were before. It's time to take a sober look at what your life was like before because disruption doesn't just destroy, it reveals. Was your "normal" sustainable, or were you holding it together with duct tape and grit?

In Step Three of the Momentum Method, we'll work to rediscover your identity after loss, clarify your values, and reclaim your voice so you can begin to live a life that actually fits.

WHO AM I NOW?

After a script break, there's typically a gap between what happened and what happens next. In that space, you have to find a way forward, but that rarely happens in a straight line. You'll often fall back on habits and behaviors that worked in the past. In Step Three, you'll start to identify those actions and find ways to move past them.

Productivity as Protection

For me, I always prided myself on being dependable, getting things done, overperforming, and being everyone's go-to. After each loss, I took my approved three days of bereavement leave and came back to the office, attending all scheduled meetings and making my to-do lists like nothing had happened.

After all, I didn't want to let anyone down.

I immediately jumped back into my color-coded calendar full of meetings, activities, practices, and games. My mind was cluttered, and my calendar became my safety net. Every minor task had a slot, because if it was written down, I didn't have to sit with my thoughts.

To me, being dependable meant:

- Saying yes, no matter what.
  Need help on a committee? Of course, I had the time. (I didn't.) Volunteer for the project? I can do it. (I couldn't.)

- Showing up, even when I didn't feel like it.
  I'd smile, act engaged, and push through, no matter how I felt internally.

- Overperforming tasks.
  If I were asked to create a meeting agenda, I'd also include an icebreaker, a notes page, and an attendance list.

- Being everyone's go-to.
  If there was a gap, a last-minute need, or a crisis, I would step in immediately.

Filling my days and spare time became a coping mechanism. If I stayed busy, I didn't have to face what was underneath.

The Breaking Point

Taking care of all these tasks and people started to make me feel resentful toward my work, then toward my friends and family... and then toward myself. I was angry because I was prioritizing everyone else's needs over my own and filling my days with things that didn't feel important to me. Even the smallest task began to feel heavy, and it felt as if I was moving in slow motion. Before I knew it, weeks blurred into months, and my resentment grew. I didn't like the person I had become.

Bitterness began to seep into everything. Writing a simple email felt like a daunting task. An invitation from a friend felt like a burden rather than a joy. I began withdrawing, not just from others, but from myself. The things that had brought me joy — reading, painting, and yoga — sat untouched.

What scared me was how numb I felt. I wasn't just overwhelmed and tired; I was disconnected. I couldn't pinpoint the last time I had felt proud of myself. Every day felt like a performance.

When everything you've built your identity on starts to crumble, you're left with one question: Who am I now?

WHAT YOU CHOOSE: MARK'S STORY

As I began to grapple with my own sense of self, I remembered a moment when my brother Mark had asked the very same question. His story is a powerful reminder that even after unimaginable loss, it's possible to find your way back to yourself, not by returning to who you were, but by discovering who you are becoming.

When Silence Took Over

My brother Mark has endured more loss than most can imagine. Technically, Mark is my biological uncle — my biological mother Lisa's brother — but because my maternal grandparents adopted me when I was a baby, he's always been my brother in every way that matters.

The greatest heartbreak came when he lost his sister, Lisa, and her husband, Mike — my parents. After their deaths, Mark withdrew from the world. For five years, he lived in a fog, consumed by grief and guilt. He told me that during that time, he didn't care about much of anything, until one Saturday, when he found himself sitting alone in his house in the dark: no lights, no TV, no sound. Just silence.

In that silence, something shifted. Suddenly, it hit him like a brick: *Why am I doing this? This isn't me.*

Turning Point

That moment changed everything. Mark realized that five years had passed since my parents' death, and he couldn't remember much that had happened in that time. He had been surviving, not living. That realization was a turning point. "After a tragedy," he told me, "you can hit rock bottom, or you can choose to move forward."

Mark chose to move forward. He told me, "You honor those you lose with memories, both good and bad. Every tragedy gives you the ability to understand others who are going through their own."

STEP 3 – GET BACK TO YOU

When our dad (my grandfather) began to decline, Mark was the one who took him to nearly every appointment, test, and hospital visit. They were always close, working together at various jobs throughout their lives. Since I lived so far away, Mark took the role of making sure that Dad got to where he needed to go and that nothing was missed. When he took him to the hospital the final time, it was devastating. Then, just seven months later, we lost Mom, and the grief doubled back on itself.

Mark's life has been marked by loss, but also by creativity. He's a talented singer, songwriter, and performer, and over the years, has performed in a variety of bands. In his twenties, he wrote and performed with a group called *The Midnight Cowboys*, then *Musgrave and Chapman*, followed by *Loose Luther, Blind Men Driving, Deuces Wild,* and finally *DoubleWide Debris*, which he formed with his son (my nephew), Keith, and a few close friends. *DoubleWide Debris* performed original songs that Mark and the band wrote, and it was a dream fulfilled.

They found real success on the Americana circuit, earning a devoted following with songs that climbed the charts. They released six albums and toured through the South and Midwest. Their music was known for its honest, soulful storytelling, rooted in lived experience.

As the years went on, Mark's health began to decline, and he realized he couldn't keep traveling and performing. He told me he played longer than he should have, and when it came time to sit his bandmates down to tell them he couldn't continue, it was, as he said, "One of the hardest things he's ever had to do."

Music had been part of his identity for decades, and when he could no longer play, he stopped writing too. "For me," he said, "writing and playing were one and the same. If I couldn't do one, I couldn't do the other."

A Different Kind of Quiet

That's when the quiet began again, but this time, it led to rediscovery. Mark has always been an artist. He used to paint and sketch, though it had been a long time since he picked up a brush. He began painting again, at first just for himself, something peaceful and creative. Then he began sharing his work with friends and family. Inspiration led him online, where he found other artists on YouTube and, later, on TikTok Live, painting together in real time. He joined chats, encouraging other painters and asking questions. Before long, others were asking him to paint with them.

What started as small connections grew into a real community where artists from all over the country paint together, have virtual coffee, and check in with each other during the week. They've held fundraisers for fellow artists, hosted art auctions to support each other, and created a space where no one feels alone. They have built something real and proved that connection isn't about proximity; it's about presence.

Today, Mark has thousands of followers, and he paints live multiple times a week. When I can't reach him by phone, I log onto TikTok, where I know I'll find him, brush in hand, creating something new. (You can find him at @mctc4evr.)

He told me, "When I paint, I can go anywhere. My body might be limited, but I go to the places I paint, even if I can't travel there in real life." His paintings are emotional; each tells a story, and in creating them, he's found his way back to himself.

Mark's story embodies what it means to *get back to you*. He's experienced heartbreak, divorce, health challenges, and loss, but through art, he's found something magical. He didn't rebuild the life he had before; he created a new one that fits the life he's living now.

STEP 3 – GET BACK TO YOU

Watching Mark rebuild reminds me that purpose doesn't come from what you've lost; it comes from what you choose to hold onto. Those choices are your compass.

GETTING BACK TO YOU

Disruption has a way of eliminating what's unnecessary, and that's when your core values emerge. Core values aren't goals or a to-do list. They're the very essence of who you are and act as your compass when a path forward isn't clear.

> *Disruption has a way of eliminating what's unnecessary, and that's when your core values emerge.*

Moving forward can get tricky when you are living between past values and not-yet-clear future values. During these in-between times, it helps to remember that your values inevitably change after a major script break. They have to. You aren't who you once were, and you may realize you don't have to be the person you thought you should be, according to others or the world.

In these moments, when everything else is stripped away, you have the chance to examine your life and values. You can make specific choices to establish who you are and who you want to become. Identifying your core values and choosing to rebuild your life around them is the most important part of Step Three and getting back to you.

Choosing With Intention

When you establish who you are and know your priorities, it's easier to make life choices that meet your needs.

For instance, when Selena Gomez was experiencing personal and health struggles, she decided to step away from her busy career to focus on her mental health. Her documentary, *My Mind & Me*, is a look at the pressure she felt to be everything to everyone.

Eventually, she had to step back and ask herself: What did she really want? What did she need? She took a break to reassess her life and goals and eventually opened Wondermind, a company focused on mental health.[7] Wondermind is an easy, inclusive space where people can come together and explore, discuss, and navigate their feelings. The main focus is on mental fitness, which includes practice, tools, and conversations.

Mel Robbins famously teaches her 5 Second Rule, a concept she created after realizing she couldn't continue saying yes to everyone and everything. She created this rule as a simple strategy to combat doubt, fear, and hesitation. The rule is: Once you have an impulse to act on a goal, you must act within five seconds, before your brain has a chance to stop you. When you have an inspiration, count down 5-4-3-2-1-GO, to keep the mind focused so it can't make excuses. Once you hit GO, act immediately because physical action changes your physiology.[8]

Each of these women chose to live by alignment, not expectation. They didn't bounce back; they rebuilt forward.

Live by alignment, not expectation.

CHECK-IN: DEFINE WHAT YOU WANT

The first step toward defining who you are at this moment involves setting and understanding your boundaries and defining what you want.

Think about your beliefs. Which ones feel true and which ones no longer work? What things were part of your old script and don't match your new focus? For instance, you could decide that you're going to protect your time by being careful about saying yes. You'll have to work on saying no, even if in the past you didn't want to let people down.

Take some time now to reflect on your life and write your answers to the following questions:

- What drains you?
- What feels like a *should* instead of a *want*?
- What no longer fits?
- What do you not want to do anymore?
- What do you dread?
- What do you enjoy?

This task isn't indulgent; it's essential. This is the foundation for momentum. You can't build forward in a life that doesn't fit.

Your Own Way Forward

When you answer these questions and begin living according to your values, not everyone will understand. Your friends, family, and colleagues may question you and wonder why you have made a huge shift in your life.

Remember, your values and choices are your own. Defining what you want is a solo project, not a group project. The people who truly care about you will understand and adjust. The people who don't? They are revealing their own priorities.

My Shift in Values

I was surprised by the outcome of my script break. If you had asked me, I would have said my life was grounded in my values. But looking back, I can see that many of them weren't really my values after all. They were molded by what others expected of me. I thought my worth depended on how much I produced, how many people I pleased, and how well I performed.

Let's compare. My values before the Momentum Method were:

- Approval
- Achievement
- Productivity
- Reliability
- Control
- Busyness

After loss and disruption stripped away what didn't matter, my values shifted and became less about *doing* and more *being*:

- Freedom
- Health
- Connection
- Creativity
- Peace

IT'S NOT ABOUT BOUNCING BACK

Getting back to you isn't about reverting to the person you were before. Instead, you are honoring the person you have become. Your disruption has changed your priorities and values, revealing what matters the most. When you know your values, you can start making intentional decisions. These decisions will help you build a life that fits — not the one others expect, but the one that is authentically yours.

You're not bouncing back, you're rebuilding forward.

REFLECTION:

Reconnecting with Yourself

When I was working to get back to myself after my losses, I started by simply writing my values in a list. I began with a "brain dump" and wrote down everything I valued. I worked on the list a little bit at a time over several days.

Now, I want you to write your own values list. Don't edit yourself; write what comes to mind. What truly matters to you? No one will read this list but you.

Here are some prompts to help you, but don't feel limited to these questions. Everyone's values are unique.

- When were you happiest in the past year?
    - What were you doing?
    - Who were you with?
- What have you started saying "no" to?
- What boundaries have you set since your disruption?
- If you could remove one recurring obligation without guilt, what would it be?
- What do you regret agreeing to? Why did you agree?

You've just completed Step Three of the Momentum Method: Get Back to You. Every rebuild deepens when you remember who you are beneath what you've lost.

CHAPTER 7

Step 4 – Dare to Dream

If you plan on being anything less than you are capable of being, you'll probably be unhappy all the days of your life.

—ABRAHAM MASLOW

Abraham Maslow's quote speaks to the idea that possibility is about living to your full potential, and that ignoring it will lead to unhappiness. However, when you're in survival mode, possibility often feels out of reach. You don't even dare to dream because dreaming feels like a luxury; an impossibility you can't afford. Instead, you focus on getting through the day and not imagining anything else.

In Step Four of the Momentum Method, we focus on finding a way back to the part of you that wants more, even if you have forgotten what "more" looks like.

WHOSE DREAM IS IT?

Disruptions throw us into survival mode, so allowing yourself to dream again can feel risky. Plus, you're embarking on a new type of dreaming that's different from what you've done in the past.

Think of it this way: Many of us have lived our daily lives following inherited roles, cultural scripts, and internal pressure. We've often met these preselected expectations, even when they're costing us our health, happiness, or sense of purpose.

Society also tells us what our dreams should be:

- **Get an education.** Whether it's a bachelor's degree or a trade school, you need an education to be successful.
- **Get a job.** You need to be employed. Even if it's not your dream job, you should be working at least 40 hours a week.
- **Work harder than everyone else.** Put in extra hours and always go above and beyond.

Society's dreams teach us to be productive, but not necessarily present. When people follow this script, they may eventually feel burned out, disconnected, or question their purpose.

While society's roadmap is practical, it's missing passion. It doesn't answer these questions: What's driving you? What do you want to do? What are you excited and passionate about? What will make you happy?

Research by sociologists Janet Ruane and Karen Cerulo shows that most Americans aren't dreaming of the American Dream.[9] Instead, they found that most of us dream of reconciling with loved ones, travelling, starting something new, or making a difference. Even when these dreams are put on hold, we don't give up on them because the act of dreaming is what gives life meaning.

STEP 4 – DARE TO DREAM

DREAMS DEFERRED

What happened to my dreams is likely what has happened to so many of you. Life simply got in the way. I was so busy taking care of family members, working full-time, being a mom, trying to be a good friend, and being a member of my community, including serving on a couple of boards. Tack on the tasks demanded in daily life (cleaning, shopping, etc.), and who has time to dream?

Our time gets taken over by everyday life, and if there's a little bit of time left, we fill it with overthinking, unreasonable expectations, and negative self-talk. It feels too risky and impractical to act on a dream. We have families that depend on us. But before we realize it, we've lived our lives without ever pursuing a dream.

Starting my own business was something I had never dared to dream. There were times I'd sketch out an idea and draft a business plan, but then I would shove it in a folder, telling myself to focus on the stability of my full-time job. I felt a mix of excitement and shame: excitement at the possibility, but shame that I wanted something different. I felt embarrassed about putting myself first at such a critical time in my son's life. I felt guilty that my finances would change drastically while I worked to build a profitable, sustainable business.

This all changed after we finished handling Jan's estate. I found myself reaching for those old folders. I couldn't continue with the status quo. I was different, and I realized I needed something different, too. I had bigger dreams. My first step was to work with my mentor, Caroline Dowd-Higgins, on an Odyssey Plan.[10] In this exercise, I wrote down three future scenarios and envisioned myself in each. Rather than running on autopilot, I considered how each plan aligned with my values and dreams, then chose a path forward.

By the time I finished my Odyssey Plan and debriefed with Caroline, the answer was clear: I would quit my current job, join my friend Dana Cummings at DSC Consulting, and start my own speaking business.

I was equal parts terrified and excited, feeling a tug-of-war between the old and new me. In the Odyssey Plan process, I went through all of the worst-case scenarios, including failure. But my dream had been pushed back too many times, and picturing myself succeeding and doing work that really excited me won out. I was still nervous, but even with the pit in my stomach, the decision was made. Now, I had to execute. I made a plan, pushed my anxiety to the side, and registered for my LLC. It was my first concrete step toward living my dream.

PURSUING YOUR DREAMS

Starting my own business fulfilled one of my dreams and moved me toward a future I was excited to create. Even though I had some doubts, I believed in myself and that dream. It's important to take these risks throughout life.

Another time when I took a chance on a dream was when I was eighteen. I dreamed of being the first person in my family to earn a bachelor's degree. It wasn't just a wish; it felt like a leap. I knew it would take long hours, hard work, and financial help to make it possible.

My first step was applying for a scholarship from the local community college. When I won, it felt like the door to my dream was opening. While attending, I worked as a bank teller. I thrived in the fast-paced, professional environment. I loved my colleagues, my customers, and the challenge. I began to grow confident that I could succeed beyond what I had previously imagined.

STEP 4 – DARE TO DREAM

Two years later, I wanted to transfer to the University of Southern Indiana, but I was concerned about how I would afford the tuition. I worked full-time the summer before and completed all the necessary loan documents. I was worried about the financial impact of this dream on both my family and me.

One day, out of the blue, Dr. Mike Dreith, the president of Frontier Community College, told me that an anonymous benefactor, someone who knew my parents and the sacrifices they had made, was giving me enough to pay my tuition for the next two years. I couldn't believe someone was willing to invest in my dreams.

That unexpected gift meant I only needed a small loan for books, housing, and a meal plan. More importantly, it was proof that my dream mattered. I wasn't just chasing an education; I was stepping into a future that I believed in, even when I doubted myself.

DREAMING AFTER DISRUPTION

Disruption can make your world feel small, but changing what you dare to believe is possible. It's time to give yourself permission to imagine a future that isn't limited by what you lost, where you came from, or what others expect from you. Many others have overcome these challenges, and you can too.

Oprah Winfrey is one of the most recognizable names in the world, but her story didn't begin with glamour and success. She grew up in poverty in rural Mississippi, survived abuse, and was raised by her grandmother. The script handed to her by circumstance was turbulent and didn't include becoming a household name.

Oprah started work in a small local television station but dreamed of creating a large platform. Her dreams eventually led her to host *The Oprah Winfrey Show*, one of the most influential talk shows in history. She's built an empire that includes media, publishing, and philanthropy. When her show ended, she created an entire network called OWN (Oprah Winfrey Network).[11] Oprah dared to dream beyond disruption.

Similarly, Academy Award winner Viola Davis has spoken openly about growing up in extreme poverty in Rhode Island. She talks about how she and her siblings grew up in rat-infested apartments and were always hungry. She often speaks about how shame and survival were themes in her childhood.[12]

In high school, Viola discovered acting through a federal program, Upward Bound.[13] I was also in Upward Bound, and I know firsthand what a difference it can make. The program is designed to help first-generation college students learn about community colleges and universities. Each summer, students are bused to local community colleges where they take classes. Some of the classes count for college credit, while others are designed to prepare students for advanced math, foreign languages, and other subjects.

The classes I took were interactive and fun, and I was surrounded by teens from across several counties whom I had never met before. At the end of the summer, we capped it off with a big trip together to the 1996 Olympics in Atlanta, Georgia. We watched a baseball game, an experience I'll never forget!

Upward Bound expanded my world and showed me possibilities I couldn't have imagined before, planting the seeds for bigger dreams. This program speaks to the power of opportunity; I learned to dream beyond what I thought possible.

Armed with the knowledge Upward Bound gave her, Viola enrolled at Rhode Island University. Her family couldn't afford tuition, so she relied on financial aid, scholarships, and work study. She discovered her love of theater at there, and ultimately, it became her major.

After graduating in 1988, Viola won a scholarship to Juilliard's drama program in New York City. Even with her scholarship, it was still difficult. She would often go hungry to afford living in New York but never gave up on her dreams. Eventually, Viola earned an Emmy, an Academy Award, and two Tony Awards. Her story is a reminder that dreams can take root, even in the hardest soil.

Like Oprah and Viola, Tyler Perry faced poverty and hardship growing up. He grew up with a violent father who abused him and his mother, and he has spoken about how much he longed to see his mother happy.[14] The rare moments he saw her light up were at church, a stark contrast to the heaviness at home. Those glimpses of joy were proof that even in the hardest times, something good can break through.[15]

Tyler carried that spark into his early career, where he wrote plays while working odd jobs and living in his car. Today, he owns one of the largest film production studios in the United States. His story shows what's possible when you believe that joy and hope exist and build a life that reflects it.

DARE TO DREAM

Your story and mine likely don't look like these, but the principle is the same. You can write a script shaped not by survival, but by possibility. You may think your dreams are too small or that it's too late. It isn't.

Returning to the Abraham Maslow quote that started this chapter, he pushes us not to settle for less than we're capable of. This means we need to notice moments when we shrink ourselves or stay where it feels safe. When this happens, the work is to keep moving forward.

You don't lose the lessons of your life when you allow yourself to imagine new dreams. It isn't disloyal to your past to dream about your future. You carry it with you and build on it.

> *It isn't disloyal to your past to dream about your future. You carry it with you and build on it.*

Give yourself permission to imagine what's possible, both big and small. Those dreams become the foundation for what comes next: rewriting your script.

REFLECTION:

Purposeful Imagining

Before getting started with purposeful imagining, set aside some time when you won't be distracted. Perhaps you prefer to sit in your bedroom with the lights off, maybe it's easier for you to do on your evening walk, or perhaps it's best done early in the morning. In any case, find a peaceful spot where you can focus.

Purposeful imagining is the conscious act of creating and focusing on images, experiences, and ideas with a specific goal in mind. It's a time to silence the inner critic who tells you what's not possible and think about what you want.

This isn't daydreaming just to daydream; it's intentionally picturing what you'd like your future to look like.

Let's start with an unedited, unfiltered brainstorming session. Let yourself imagine, without judging yourself, and dream about what's possible, not practical. Sometimes the simplest questions are the most revealing.

- What do I daydream about?
- If I could do something just for joy, what would it be?
- What dream visits you on a walk, in the shower, or in the car?
- What is possible if you stop asking permission, both from others and from yourself?

Big Dreams and Small Dreams

Now, get two pieces of paper and label one "small dreams" and the other "big dreams." I like to define them as follows:

- **Small dreams** often have immediate next steps and can feel modest (but are still meaningful), such as taking a class, reaching out to an old friend, starting a garden, or reading more books.
- **Big dreams** are longer-term projects that require vision and courage to step into the unknown. These are dreams like changing careers, writing a book, launching a business, or even traveling abroad.

Small dreams give us momentum; big dreams provide us with direction. Both matter!

Next, take a moment to review your answers to the Purposeful Imagining questions and decide which category you'd put them in. Don't allow yourself time to question them; just write. Give your imagination space to breathe. Maybe you'll even come up with some new ones.

> *Small dreams give us momentum; big dreams provide us with direction. Both matter!*

Sharing My Dreams

I did this exercise before I decided to leave my job, launch my own business, and join my friend Dana at her consulting firm. It took me a few weeks to get all my thoughts on paper and allow myself to process what I had written.

Seeing my dreams on paper made me feel a mix of emotions: overwhelmed, excited, and filled with possibility. The pages were messy, full of scribbles, notes in the margins, and ink in all different colors. You have permission to be messy in this process. Messiness often leads to success.

The beauty in dreams is that you don't have to do it all alone. As you go through the process, talk with trusted sources who

STEP 4 – DARE TO DREAM

will be honest sounding boards. While dreaming of my future, I had lengthy discussions with my husband, my brother Mark, my best friend Andrea, and my mentor, Caroline. They all offered different perspectives and challenged me in different ways.

> **You've just completed Step Four of the Momentum Method: Dare to Dream. Every rebuild expands when you give yourself permission to imagine what could be next.**

CHAPTER 8

Step 5 – Rewrite Your Script

You either learn your way towards writing your own script in life, or you unwittingly become an actor in someone else's script.

—JOHN TAYLOR GATTO

Every day, we make choices about how to live our lives. When we don't actively make those choices and write our own script, someone else will inevitably do it for us. After all the work you've done, that's no longer an option.

Think of this final step of the Momentum Method as the moment when the curtain rises. You understand what came before. You've prepared yourself, and now it's time to decide how this story continues and ends.

DEFAULT SCRIPTS

Many of us follow the goals our parents, society, or others have set for us, but when their dreams take the place of our own, we end up living their story instead of ours.

In this way, scripts are powerful, not because they are true, but because they feel true. Without realizing it, we recreate the same dynamics again and again.

An article in *The Guardian*, "The Meaning of Life Scripts," calls these unconscious life scripts, patterns shaped in childhood that influence us throughout our lives.[16] It's important to understand these narratives so we can challenge and rewrite them.

The themes can be destructive, such as "People always leave," or "I'm not good enough," or even "Bad things always happen to me." However, sometimes our scripts can seem positive but contain destructive elements, such as "I always need to succeed" or "I can't rest until everyone else is happy." These scripts can be harder to spot because, on the surface, they sound good, but in reality, they set unattainable goals.

Family scripts can run particularly deep. For instance, if your family's unspoken rule was to not make waves, then you likely learned to stay quiet and keep the peace, even when it meant hiding your opinions. This kind of inherited script may feel like a part of who you are, but is it? It may no longer align with the life you want to live.

These examples illustrate ways of living inside someone else's script and living lives handed to us long ago that we mistake for truth. Now is the time to look at your life and decide where your script is headed.

Colliding Scripts

Most of us don't realize our script may contain default scripts that we've followed for so long that we don't even question them. But a disruption forces us to take notice.

Like many of you, my script was created as a child. It stemmed from losing my biological parents and my grandparents adopting me. Because they adopted me when they were older and had already been through so much, I tried not to upset them or cause any trouble. I felt a responsibility to be the perfect child, one who never disobeyed.

This script grew and became "Andrea the achiever, the fixer, and the one who never lets anyone down." I was a model rule-follower, agonizing over grades and perfection, chastising myself for even small mistakes. Any failure felt like I was letting everyone down. I put a lot of pressure on myself to live up to the script I thought I needed to follow.

When my husband and I adopted our son when he was twelve, I carried my old script right into motherhood: I wanted to be the perfect parent. He had already known trauma, experienced abandonment, and lived with PTSD, so I felt like I needed to earn the right to be his mom. That pressure was heavy. I read every book I could find on parenting teenagers, followed advice from my friends, and modeled my own mother's style.

Ultimately, our two scripts collided. His script carried trauma, distrust, and the need for safety. My script was built on perfection and performance, and it wouldn't let me redefine what motherhood could look like. While he needed space and unconditional acceptance, I was busy trying to create a life that looked perfect. Our scripts clashed, and this often made me feel anxious and misunderstood.

Chances are, you have experienced a collision of scripts as a parent, in a relationship, or even at work. We bring our expectations into relationships, only to find they don't fit the reality of the other person's story. That's why rewriting matters. We don't want to keep repeating the same lines we were given if they don't serve the people we love or us.

As a caregiver for my family and husband, I wanted to remain upbeat and positive while keeping all the balls in the air. Appointments made, house cleaned, dinner on the table, and working a full-time job. I could do it all. I wasn't allowed to fall apart. I wanted to be the perfect caregiver, but that is unsustainable.

Everyone's inherited script is shaped by their family, experiences, and life circumstances. It then impacts those around you.

What happened to me may not be what happened to you. But we've both been following scripts that we probably haven't carefully examined, and now they're quietly shaping how we behave, think, and choose.

My script kept me functioning while everything else was falling apart. I followed it faithfully until I began to collide with those I loved, and I started to resent it.

What scripts are you still following?

NAME YOUR SCRIPT

If you don't name and rewrite your script, it will keep writing itself. But rewriting begins with recognition. You need to identify and name the old script that's been running on autopilot in the background. When you stop living by lines you've memorized without even realizing it, you can begin to define your own path forward.

> *If you don't name and rewrite your script, it will keep writing itself.*

STEP 5 – REWRITE YOUR SCRIPT

Dr. Marianna Pogosyan details how naming emotions can reduce emotional stress.[17] Labeling feelings quiets the amygdala (the brain's alarm system) and activates our prefrontal cortex (the reasoning part of the brain). For example, if you say, "I feel anxious," your amygdala begins to calm. When you identify and name your script, its hold on you loosens, which gives you space to think differently and begin rewriting.

When a Script Looks Like It's Working

Naming a script can be tricky because many of them run on autopilot. They're patterns we've followed for such a long time that we barely notice them. Some even appear as positive, rewarding us with success, achievement, or approval. But beneath the surface, these seemingly helpful scripts can have a darker cost.

Consider the following scripts:

- *I have to succeed, no matter what.*
  On the surface, this appears to celebrate ambition. It also causes burnout, perfectionism, and an inability to rest.

- *It's my job to keep everyone happy.*
  This sounds like kindness. Don't we all want to make our family, friends, and colleagues happy? It may seem natural, but when it's woven into your script, it can lead to people-pleasing, resentment, and even loss of self.

- *I don't need help; I can handle it.*
  Have you heard the phrase, "Many hands make light work"? Yes, you may be able to handle it, but at what cost? It may appear to be independence, but it actually isolates you and blocks out support.

What scripts in your life have earned you praise or rewards, but also left you feeling burned out, exhausted, and even resentful?

It's easy to confuse these false positives with the truth. Rewriting your script doesn't mean that you can't be successful, kind, and independent. But wouldn't your script read better if it were healthier and more genuine? You deserve a script that aligns with your values, rather than one that lets the past have the final word.

REWRITE YOUR SCRIPT

Now that you can identify and name your default scripts, the real work begins. Rewriting your script means deciding what stays, what changes, and what no longer gets to stick around. You're setting a new course shaped by intention rather than habit.

The rewriting process rarely follows a standard path. The process takes time and courage, but the result is worth it. You'll begin living a life that aligns with your script and moves you forward.

Progress Isn't Linear

Rewriting your script doesn't mean a clean or easy break. It often looks like a series of brave decisions made in the middle of uncertainty. My good friend, Katie, embodies this kind of metamorphosis where you keep moving forward despite not having all the answers.

I met Katie at work. She had been with the organization for sixteen years. Her job felt familiar, predictable, and safe, but deep down, she knew it was no longer where she was meant to stay.

The decision to rewrite her script had been brewing quietly for a long time, but suddenly, Katie couldn't shake the feeling that change was calling. She had just left a toxic relationship and could see that the story she was living no longer matched who she was becoming.

Then, not long after, everything shifted. A lightbulb moment made her realize it might finally be time to move on, and she made a bold choice. She quit her job after sixteen years and decided to move five hours away to a different state.

Katie sold her house, packed up her life, and moved. Her first job wasn't quite right, but instead of seeing that as a failure, she recognized it wasn't aligned with her long-term goals and found another opportunity that better fit her passion.

Katie has always been drawn to human resources; she's a natural at policy development, compliance, and one-on-one relationships. With the encouragement of a mentor who believed in her, she began to believe in herself. Her mentor helped her quiet the negative self-talk that was holding her back and helped her see her strengths with confidence.

Today, Katie is thriving both professionally and personally. She's in a new relationship that brings her joy, working at a job that challenges her, and living a life that finally feels like *hers*.

Katie reminds me that courage doesn't always roar; sometimes it's found in the quiet decision to begin again, even when you don't know what comes next.

Scribbling In The Margins

Another powerful rewrite belonged to my friend and colleague, Dana. For years, she worked in leadership roles that appeared fulfilling from the outside: meaningful work, a respected title, and a team she deeply cared about.

But over time, the environment around her began to change, and what had once been challenging became heavy. The more things changed around her, the more she began to question whether this version of success still fit who she was.

She thought she'd wait for the "right" moment to make a change, but the right opportunity never came. Eventually, she reached the point where she couldn't keep going. She was exhausted and depleted, and she knew something had to change. Staying was no longer an option.

We had breakfast one Saturday morning, and she shared what she was wrestling with. I reminded her of what she already knew: She could do anything, and she would be successful anywhere. She later told me how that conversation helped her find the courage to leave, even though she didn't know what would come next.

It was a brave decision. She walked away, not because she had another plan in place, but because she knew in her gut that it was time to move on.

In the months that followed, she completed her doctorate and created DSC Consulting, doing work that felt aligned, creative, and meaningful. She continues to build a life that's defined by choice, not circumstance. I joined her at DSC in August 2025, one of the best decisions I've ever made.

> *Build a life that's defined by choice, not circumstance.*

Dana conveyed that one of the best things about getting older is that you stop apologizing for wanting more. You become choosier and stop settling for environments that aren't working for you or don't see your worth. You also realize that walking away isn't giving up; it's choosing to begin again, but this time on your own terms.

Dana often shares that we do ourselves a disservice by following only one playbook for our careers, like the belief that you can't leave a job until you have another lined up. Sometimes the rewrite begins when you step outside the rules everyone else is following and trust that your next chapter will take shape as you go.

Her story reminds me that rewriting your script doesn't always look like a clean page. Sometimes it's a courageous decision scribbled in the margins, a moment when you decide to stop surviving what isn't working and start creating what will. Dana's story proves that rewriting your script doesn't require a complete life overhaul; it can begin with admitting, "This isn't who I am anymore."

Katie and Dana's stories are reminders that rewriting your script isn't reserved for celebrities or public figures; it's something ordinary people do every day in extraordinary ways. But sometimes, those truths show up on a much bigger stage.

REWRITING IN PUBLIC

Some rewrites play out quietly; others unfold in full view. Whether the change is public or private, the courage to start again is the same.

Robert Downey Jr.'s story shows how deeply embedded scripts can be rewritten, even when the world is watching. He's had a long battle with drug addiction. He was brought up in a home where drug use was normalized, creating a script from childhood that told him, "Everybody does drugs; it's normal." His addiction began when he was just six years old, and his father, a filmmaker who cast Downey in a small role, gave him marijuana. Downey has said, "There was always a lot of pot and coke around… When my dad and I would do drugs together, it was like him trying to express his love for me in the only way he knew how." This furthered his script, adding that "love and drugs go together" and "self-destruction is part of success." By eight years old, Downey said he would "spend every night out getting drunk and making a thousand phone calls in pursuit of drugs."[18]

As he got older, following this script cost him everything that mattered, including his career, his reputation, and his relationships. He was all over the headlines, and everyone was reading about his erratic behavior, being late to sets, and a one-year prison term. He went to rehab several times but never believed a script that said he was worth it.

In 2003, the year he met his wife, he realized, "I don't think I can do this anymore," and he finally got sober. To do this, he had to completely change his life script to "I am worthy of love and success without substances." He was unemployable due to a hefty insurance premium he couldn't afford. His good friend, fellow actor Mel Gibson, cast him in a movie and paid the insurance premium. From there, he began to receive more work, and his star was on the rise. Within five years, he starred as Tony Stark in *Iron Man*, which was the start of the multibillion-dollar Marvel Universe.[19]

Downey's old script told him that chaos was love, and drugs were normal. When he rewrote his script, he discovered that love is a source of stability and that purpose is more powerful than addiction. With his wife and friends supporting him, he was able to rewrite a script that is still true today. He is sober, working, and living a life that has purpose.

Tracee Ellis Ross has often spoken about the extreme pressure to live up to her mother's career while trying to make her own place in Hollywood. For years, she was overlooked and undervalued as an actress.

Fueled by passion and wanting to be known for her accolades instead of her mother's, she rewrote her script. She built her career, starting with *Girlfriends* and later with an Emmy-winning role on *Black-ish*. She also founded a hair company, Pattern, which celebrates natural hair. She rewrote her script.[20]

None of us is bound by our families or external expectations. It doesn't matter what the world says your script is; you have the power to control your own script and rewrite it at any time.

STEP 5 – REWRITE YOUR SCRIPT

It's likely your story doesn't involve fame, but have you been cast in the background because of family, work, or circumstance? You don't have to stick with that narrative; you get to write a script that has you in the leading role.

Rewriting isn't just about words; it's about you stepping into your new role, even if you are still growing into it. This won't happen overnight, but recognizing the old scripts that are holding you back is the only way to rebuild forward.

REFLECTION:

Begin the Rewrite

We've moved through all the Momentum Method steps, and now, it's time to rewrite your script so you can live a life that suits you. It doesn't need outside validation, and you can choose what you want next.

You know what your script should be. Trust what you already know. You will stumble and repeat old patterns. That's not failure; it's rebuilding forward. Remember, imperfect action counts. Rewriting your script isn't quick or easy; it's a process.

What I've detailed below is a before-and-after reflection tool that allows you to see your own arc.

- **Your Old Script**
  This is what you followed before the disruption because it felt safe and familiar, even if it wasn't healthy.
    - How was your script created?
    - What rules or expectations formed your script?
    - What about your old script felt comfortable but not quite right?
    - Does your script honor your values?
    - Are there components of your script that are working, and you want to keep?

- **The Script Break**
  This is the moment your story was shattered. Perhaps it was death, a divorce, a job loss, or a diagnosis. What was the turning point that made you realize your old script wasn't going to work?
    - When was the moment your story shattered?

STEP 5 – REWRITE YOUR SCRIPT

- How did that moment change you?
- What were the first signs that your current script couldn't continue?

- **The Struggle**
  The moment your story shatters and the time immediately after will reveal where you are struggling. Are you struggling to follow the script because it no longer fits?
    - What parts of your old script are hard to get rid of?
    - Are you trying to hold on to that script, even when you know it isn't working?
    - Are there external pressures (family, friends, work) that are holding you back?

- **The Realization**
  It's time to face what your old script is costing you. You may have realized this slowly over time, or it may have hit you like a bolt of lightning. No matter how you came to realize it, you know it's time for a change.
    - What is your old script costing you? This could be relationships, a promotion, or starting your own business, to name a few.
    - What do you now recognize about yourself, your relationships, or your values?
    - Are you ready to let go of your old script and write a different one?

- **Time for a Rewrite**
  You have the choice to either live in your old script (a script you didn't create and doesn't honor your values) or write a new one (a script you choose and reflects what

you value). This will take time, and it's not an overnight fix, but you can do it.
- When you look at your old script, what feels true and what doesn't?
- What is driving you to rewrite your script?
- How do you want to feel when you think of your new script?
- Who are you now becoming because of your rewrite?

> **You've just completed Step Five of the Momentum Method: Rewrite Your Script. Every rebuild transformation starts when you stop waiting for your old story to return and begin writing the one you were meant to live.**

PART 3

THE WORK OF LIVING AGAIN

CHAPTER 9

Life Interrupted

After a script break, life doesn't go back to how it was. Showing up can feel hard when everything has shattered, whether by loss, a change, or an unexpected ending. In this chapter, we explore how to find your footing on hard days, while also honoring the truth that it's okay to feel what you feel.

I was lost after my Mom's death. When she was alive, I called her every morning, whether I was on the way to school, work, or running errands. I couldn't start my day with a clear mind if I didn't make sure Mom and Dad were okay.

The first morning I drove to work after Mom passed was agonizing. I tried to listen to the radio, then a podcast, and finally sat in silence, tears streaming down my cheeks. I felt hollow and empty, but when I pulled into my work parking spot, I wiped my tears, applied my lipstick, and plastered on a smile. After all, I had a busy day full of meetings and deadlines, and I needed to have it together. When I arrived at my desk, I sat down at my computer, watching my emails pile up higher and higher with each passing hour. I would open one, then close it. I couldn't focus, and the number of emails kept climbing like a silent accusation.

When you've been through a script break and it's shattered you to your core, you feel isolated, lost, and overwhelmed. You aren't sure how to get through the minute-by-minute, let alone the day or week, yet the pace of work and everyday life never slows down. You feel as though you have to keep moving and producing to stay ahead. While we often reserve the word "grief" for death, it's not the only loss that walks with us into the office.

What you are facing doesn't clock in or out; it shows up in Zoom or Teams meetings, in hallway conversations, tight smiles, and unread emails. It lingers behind deadlines and performance reviews, hiding in our silence during small talk.

Most workplaces, and the world at large, don't make space for script breaks. But living through a disruption requires new rhythms, not a return to the old pace. Emotion doesn't disappear just because your calendar has moved on.

SOCIAL EXPECTATIONS

A disconnect exists between policies and lived experience. In professional settings, there's often no vocabulary for loss and no way to say, "I'm doing my best, but my heart is elsewhere." When someone dies, you are allowed some time off. Laws vary by state, but I was allotted three days of bereavement leave and then expected to return focused, smiling, and ready to go.

Logistically, three days doesn't give you enough time to contact family and prepare the funeral. The draining phone calls spent telling everyone the devastating news are followed by funeral planning that ranges from writing the obituary and selecting a funeral home to picking out a loved one's burial outfit and organizing a service you never wanted to plan.

There are countless things to do, and you are doing them while grieving and feeling physical pain, sickness, and heartbreak that is unlike anything you have previously known.

Policy Shift

Some companies are beginning to realize this disconnect and are changing their policies to accommodate more realistic timelines. Meta recently doubled its bereavement leave to twenty days for the death of an immediate family member and ten days for an extended family member. For companies without these policies, the Society for Human Resource Management has found that 30 percent of employees use sick or vacation days after the loss of a loved one.[21]

Bereavement is only one example of how life-changing events collide with work expectations. When a relationship ends, there isn't an official leave policy, but the loss will shape your day and your work.

Statistically, 42 percent of marriages end in separation, and there is often no allotted time given for this traumatic event. A study by Rayden Solicitors found that 79 percent of employees felt their divorce had an impact on their ability to work. A study conducted by the Nashville Business Journal found that employee productivity decreases by 40 percent during the first six months of a divorce.[22]

Grief, of any sort, tends to be nonlinear and recurring. There will be triggers that remind you of what happened, and it's important to honor your feelings.

Unseen Losses

These statistics don't account for the many other devastating script breaks that happen during our lives. The loss of a job doesn't come with casseroles or sympathy cards, but it still shakes you to your core, just like the loss of a beloved pet. Many of us are grieving the loss of the life we imagined, whether it's a career that stalled, a diagnosis that changed everything, or even an anniversary of an event that rolls around — the date of someone's death or when a divorce was finalized.

These losses don't always come with leave, but they affect us just as deeply.

PERSONAL EXPECTATIONS

Sometimes we return to work because, when everything else has changed, it hasn't. Familiar routines and clear expectations can feel safe — a way to keep busy and avoid what hurts. The problem with this timeline is that unspoken grief can become chronic exhaustion, detachment, and burnout.

After losing my father-in-law, Dad, Mom, and my mother-in-law, I took my allotted three days of bereavement for each of them and went right back to work because I thought I had to. Responsibility and following the rules were part of my script, and I didn't even consider another option. To me, being dependable felt safer than allowing myself to be human and to deal with real, very raw emotions. I also didn't want to let my colleagues down.

The emails and deadlines didn't stop just because I was going through a crisis. I didn't want to be judged by others for taking too long. Plus, I told myself I needed to stay busy, and I needed the distractions of work. The world often rewards stoic professionalism but not vulnerability.

I kept my emotions in check at work and remained professional. Even when my world had changed, the expectations around me stayed exactly the same. I cried in the privacy of my office or the bathroom, but I was always one of the first to arrive at work in my department. Something was soothing about entering the hallway when it was completely dark and quiet. I turned on the lights, started the coffee, and was able to breathe before the day's chaos began.

If I could go back, I would have taken more time, because grief is hard. Although the world pushes us to "keep going," you have to assess what that means for *you*. The clock may say it's time to move on, but the heart is still learning how to carry what's been lost.

Whether it's the loss of someone we love or the life we imagined, grief changes us and how we move through the world. This applies not just after a funeral, but also after a quiet ending that no one else saw — the loss of a dream, a relationship, or a version of life you thought you'd be living. These losses are rarely acknowledged, but they still accompany us to work.

Honor What Matters

When going through a major life disruption, your priorities and values will change. You will view the world from a different perspective and work in a different way. Even when the world doesn't give you space, you will need to create your own boundaries and rhythms. You don't have to justify what matters to you; you just need to honor it.

> *You don't have to justify what matters to you; you just need to honor it.*

Grief, of any sort, makes us question whether our needs are necessary (taking time off, seeing a counselor, asking for a reduction in workload). The world may want justification for any accommodations, but healing requires you to give yourself permission to meet your needs.

I began seeing a grief counselor after Mom died, and I agonized over taking the time off work. It was a thirty-minute drive to the appointment, a one-hour appointment, and a thirty-minute drive back. It's important to note that my boss fully supported this and never made me feel guilty about taking the time. However, I beat myself up about it. I felt guilty for leaving work and taking time for something that felt indulgent. It was only after several sessions that I began to really see the value in going and how important it was to allow myself the space to attend.

Your grief doesn't run on deadlines. You need to release the pressure to make it go faster and stick to your timeline because it simply won't change.

Gentle Structure

I know what it's like to start a hectic day with a to-do list that's a mile long and not even know where to start. It's overwhelming, like a wet blanket on you, making it hard to breathe. It feels like your brain has short-circuited, and your energy is depleted. There were several times when I was so overwhelmed by my lists and all that was going on that I would start the day with my palms sweating, my breath shallow, and my heart racing.

I didn't want anyone at work to question my productivity, and I needed a way to grieve while keeping all the balls in the air. What got me through wasn't big or fancy; it was something as simple as making a detailed list. I began using detailed lists to give my brain a place to rest and refocus. It helped me to reclaim focus and prioritize, while still giving myself a chance to breathe.

Here is what worked for me: Write down whatever you need to do — at work, home, grocery lists, anything on your mind that you need to do. Don't edit yourself, just write it all down.

Once everything is out of your head and on paper, you can begin to bring order to the chaos.

From the first dump of information, you can begin to sort your list into smaller categories: today, this week, soon, and later. Keep these lists separate so that you can focus solely on the 'today' list. Because I love crossing things off, I break tasks into small steps. Every thick black line through a task gives me relief.

Here is where I take it one step further (this is my favorite part!). I break down my 'today' list into micro steps. Tiny wins add up, and each one gives a little momentum back.

> **DETAILED TASK EXAMPLE: PREPARING FOR A DOCTOR'S APPOINTMENT**
>
> - Write down on a note card any symptoms or issues you would like to discuss with your doctor.
> - Make sure you have your insurance card and ID.
> - Have an updated list of your current medications and dosage instructions.
> - Make sure the appointment is on your calendar.
> - Set alarms on your phone for one hour and another for thirty minutes before you need to leave.

This may seem simple, but when your head and heart aren't in sync, detailed lists mean you don't have to remember everything all at once.

You can use this same structure for any task, whether it's prepping for a board meeting, planning your child's birthday party, or handling household chores. This approach saved me when my mind was hazy, and I was having trouble concentrating.

Beyond the list itself, remember this: You don't have to walk into work pretending everything is fine. You have been through (and are going through) something painful and difficult. You don't need to put on a mask. Your feelings are not unprofessional. They are part of you, and you deserve grace.

CHAPTER 10

Finding Your Way Back

When life breaks our script, we don't just lose the person or dream at the center of that break; we also lose who we were in it. Every disruption, no matter its form, reshapes our sense of self. Disruption doesn't just take people or plans; it takes pieces of us. It's important to remember that this is a normal result of a script break. And in order to move forward, you have to recognize that these feelings of lost identity are valid.

After we cleaned out Mom and Dad's house, I felt like a stranger in my own life. I went through the motions, but I wasn't sure who I was anymore. My roles had always been clear: wife, daughter, caregiver, and achiever. Each of these roles gave me purpose and stability, and I was proud of them. Losing the role of daughter was harder than I ever imagined. My parents were my cornerstone, and without them, I felt like an orphan.

I kept showing up to everything, smiling and prepared, believing I could fake it until I made it. But I felt numb. I felt pressure to keep being "the strong one" and get everything done. I was exhausted, and when I looked in the mirror, I saw a hollow reflection staring back at me. The person I had been was gone, and I wasn't sure who I was becoming.

When I saw my friends, they would ask if I was okay. I always responded that I was fine, thanked them for asking, and never went any further. Some friends seemed relieved, while others saw through my mask, but they never pushed me.

I was resentful. I resented others who still had their parents and could have large family Christmas celebrations. I resented my friends who had babies while I was trying so desperately to conceive. Guilt began to layer on top of resentment, because I knew I should be happy for them, but I couldn't quite manage it. Honestly, I resented everyone who appeared to be living the life they imagined when mine had fallen apart.

IDENTITY GRIEF

When you lose someone or something, you also often lose the version of yourself that existed before the script break. This is identity grief. It can show up in many script breaks. For example, with divorce, when you lose the role of spouse and the "we" identity, you may still catch yourself saying "we" or "us" even months later. The routines that you built together no longer exist, and doing things you previously did together can be hard. You may feel lost when the holidays come around, and the old traditions you used to love are gone.

It shows up in infertility when you are mourning the identity of becoming a parent. I smiled when countless women advised me to "just relax, and it will happen," even though I knew, medically, it was impossible. I knew they meant well, but it didn't make their comments hurt less. You grieve the life you imagined as a parent, guiding and watching your child grow.

Although you are genuinely happy for your friends having children, it's hard to watch them living the life you dreamed of for yourself. Infertility grief is two-fold; you grieve both the imagined child and the imagined version of yourself as a parent.

Identity grief is common with job loss, when you are no longer identified as an employee or part of a team. You struggle with how to introduce yourself, having started with your title and position for years, and you may be at a loss when meeting new people who ask, "What do you do?" Your goals are interrupted, and you may not know where you are headed in your career. Losing a job can cause a crisis of confidence that rattles your sense of identity.

When you lose a pet and your days feel off, you are likely experiencing identity grief. The house feels quieter, and no one greets you with a wagging tail and a kiss when you come home. Suddenly, the walks, treats, and belly rubs are gone, leaving a hole in your day and routine. The unconditional love that has supported you through difficult moments is no longer there. I remember the first time I came home, and there was no greeting from my beloved Phoebe; the house felt empty, and so did my heart.

Loss of Social Identity

You don't have to actually lose a person, job, or dream to feel grief. It's not uncommon to feel grief when you experience a loss of social identity. This can happen when you leave any group, whether it be the colleagues left behind when changing jobs or when you leave volunteer groups, boards, churches, or any other group you identify with.

Dr. Vivian Ching explains that social identity is "the part of an individual's self-concept that is derived from their membership in social groups. These identities influence how we see ourselves and others, and offer a sense of belonging that drives behaviors such as loyalty, conformity, and intergroup conflict."[23]

Leaving a job means leaving the community of your colleagues. We spend hours working, laughing, and sharing our lives with our colleagues, and it's difficult to go from seeing them daily to not at all. I certainly felt this when I left Franklin College, leaving a community and colleagues I had worked with for ten years.

Any time you realize the life you imagined isn't going to work out the way you planned, you will likely experience identity grief. Perhaps it was a career path that ended, a risk that you didn't take, or a place you wanted to live, but you never had the chance. It can also be triggered when the kids leave home, it's time to retire, or you or someone you know deals with a chronic illness.

We build our sense of self around roles, relationships, and dreams. We lose a part of ourselves and what we imagined for our lives when it doesn't turn out the way we planned. That's why it feels so devastating, regardless of the specific loss.

FALSE BELIEFS THAT KEEP US STUCK

When I was young and going through something difficult, my mom used to tell me, "Somebody else has it worse." I know this was meant to toughen me up, but looking back, I realize it diminished my feelings. It taught me to minimize my pain instead of calling it like it was, and I felt guilty anytime I allowed myself to mourn. This script followed me into adulthood. I have caught myself saying the exact phrase to my son when he tells me about something, and I immediately redirect and validate his feelings.

Another false belief in the script is, "I should be further along by now." Whether in grief, job hunting, healing, or moving on, we convince ourselves that there is a universal timeline.

We look at those around us and compare ourselves to them. The truth is, we have no idea how others are coping or what is happening in their lives. We create our own narrative that makes them look good and makes us look like we're behind.

This narrative has haunted me as I've been writing this book. I look at other authors and how quickly and efficiently they wrote their books, and I feel behind, wondering what I am doing wrong. I have to remind myself that I don't know their writing schedule; perhaps they wrote until the early morning hours or missed life events to prioritize the book. I finally broke free of this by constantly reminding myself that I am moving at a pace that works for me with everything I have going on in my life, and that's okay.

Another false narrative is, "Other people would be handling this better." This one is difficult because all that most people show in their lives is the highlight reel. We post smiling, happy pictures on social media and rarely show photos of tears, sadness, or hardship. Social media affects us all, and it's hard, especially when you are going through something difficult, to log on and see all the triumphs and smiles. The truth is that no one escapes disruption, regardless of their finances, status, or achievements. It affects us all — we just don't publicize it on social media.

> *The truth is that no one escapes disruption, regardless of their finances, status, or achievements. It affects us all — we just don't publicize it on social media.*

These beliefs ignore your feelings and keep you stuck. They are full of comparison, judgment, and shame, and they chip away at your sense of self. They convince you that you are failing when you are simply living through a script break. You have to shed those beliefs to move ahead.

LOSING, THEN REFINDING MYSELF

Life was unbearably sad in the months after my mom and dad died. I worked hard to maintain the facade at work, pretending I was handling everything just fine. Truthfully, all my energy was spent at work, and by the time I got home, I was exhausted. I was holding it together for everyone else. Several people praised me for being "so strong," and in those moments, I felt proud. I now realize this is identity performance: presenting myself as the competent professional while feeling hollow inside.

A few months later, I noticed my pants were snug, and that I was getting more winded while climbing the stairs at work. My body also felt different. During yoga, the poses were challenging to get into and even harder to hold. I had once cared deeply about health and my body, but I didn't have the energy to worry about it. These physical cues became symbolic of my identity unraveling. When I looked around at others who had been through a similar loss, I noticed how much better they were doing than I was, and I felt guilty.

Although I was hitting all my deadlines and goals at work, I was losing my spark, and I knew my mom would have been disappointed in me. Her absence left me without the mirror I always looked into for validation. Without her, I wasn't sure who I was measuring myself against anymore.

One morning, I decided to weigh myself. I stepped on the scale and saw that I had gained nearly fifty pounds. I was stunned, ashamed, and embarrassed. I didn't feel like "me." I felt like a stranger. I began to prioritize walking my dogs in the morning while listening to music or a podcast. I restarted my yoga practice and resumed my healthy eating habits, while prioritizing sleep and hobbies. Slowly, the weight came off. But it hadn't just been about weight. It was about proving I could get back to myself. I could rewrite my script after loss.

Embrace the Transition

Before you can move forward, you have to acknowledge and accept that you are not the same person you were before. Give yourself permission to feel foreign in your own life; it's part of the rebuilding process. You haven't disappeared. You are just in transition. You're not broken. You are creating space for what's to come. Just like the Momentum Method, you are rebuilding, step by step. You don't build a house overnight. Rebuilding your identity takes time, patience, and a belief that all the pieces will come together.

> *Give yourself permission to feel foreign in your own life; it's part of the rebuilding process.*

REFLECTION:

What Feels Different, What Feels Familiar

Take a moment to consider your life at this moment. Then, list one part of your life that feels unfamiliar right now and one part that still feels like "you." Write a few thoughts about how you are feeling about each.

Notice that both can exist at the same time.

CHAPTER 11

Measure Your Life by Meaning

When you set down the need to do it all, you create room to ask a better question: What actually matters? How do we rebuild a life that's measured by meaning, not by output?

As we discussed earlier, our culture glorifies productivity. It often doesn't matter if the productivity has substance; what matters is being busy. It's easy to feel behind in life when you log onto social media and see what everyone else is doing. You'll see peers starting side businesses, joining boards, navigating multiple children in multiple sports and plays, attending receptions and happy hours — the list goes on and on. It makes us feel guilty if we *aren't* busy. Here's what hustle culture never acknowledges: recovery, rest, and reflection are all work too, just a different kind.

Hustle culture tells us that if we move fast enough, smile convincingly enough, and keep our schedules full enough, we can outrun pain. That's the trick of hustle culture: It convinces you that if you keep moving, no one, including yourself, will notice you are falling apart.

Hustling serves a purpose if you're hustling toward a goal, but not if you're hustling for affirmation or appearances and certainly not if you're hustling to avoid your feelings.

THE MYTH OF BUSYNESS

For many of us, busyness is worn like a proud badge, and when someone asks you how you are, we respond with late nights, endless projects, and how many activities our children are in. If being the "strong one" were a character, busyness would be its costume.

When we've experienced a script break, staying busy is often a convenient way to avoid dealing with our circumstances and feelings. There are lots of ways we try to justify this busyness.

The fuller your calendar, the more meetings you have, and the later you work, the more you prove you are succeeding, right? Ray Williams identifies reasons busyness hooks us.[24] Let's look at some of these reasons and the ways busyness is used as a crutch during a disruption. Do you see yourself in any of these busyness situations?

Badge of honor

We glorify busy. We hashtag and measure our success by being busy, but being busy doesn't always mean better. This is evident when you log onto social media and scroll. You will see hashtags like #NoDaysOff, #RiseandGrind, and even #TeamNoSleep. This is becoming even more prevalent as influencers take over social media and make millions promoting hustle. Curated social media makes us believe that everyone is "doing it all," and we should be too. Busy has become the new humblebrag.

> *Busy has become the new humblebrag.*

Society praises hustle, as evidenced by phrases like "sleep when you're dead." There is a cost associated with saying "yes" to everything, including strained relationships, missed opportunities, and fragile health due to stress and not allowing your body time to rest.

Busy might impress others, but it rarely sustains us.

Job security

It's important to do meaningful, high-quality work at your job, and there are times when putting in extra hours is necessary. Still, if you are working all the time to avoid disruption or its aftermath, you are just hiding and delaying the inevitable.

Many workplaces and supervisors still reward presence over performance. Presenteeism, defined as coming to work when sick or unable to function at full capacity, also affects burnout. Monica Wang from Boston University says, "Chronic presenteeism intensifies work-related stress and burnout. Nearly 60 percent of US workers in 2024 experienced burnout, ranging from moderate to very high."[25]

When busyness is used to measure success, both organizations and employees pay the price.

Are you staying late because your workload requires it, or is it because you're afraid that taking time to care for yourself after a script break might make you seem replaceable?

Busyness to Fill Time

We have countless ways to fill our time, leaving no quiet moments. We often use busyness to avoid silence.

Many of us struggle to sit with our thoughts; I'm certainly guilty of this. When everything stops, our emotions have room to surface, and that can be uncomfortable or even overwhelming.

For me, sitting quietly meant feeling sad and lonely, emotions I didn't want to acknowledge. Staying busy gave me a way to drown those feelings out. The more I filled my days, the less space there was for grief to catch up with me.

THE COST OF DOING IT ALL

We're often praised for being "the strong one," the one who can hold it all together. The times I have been praised most often were when I was only pretending I had figured it out.

My husband has had twenty-three surgeries, six of those since we've been married, and each and every time, I've refused help from friends and family. They always ask how they can help lessen the load, but I tell them that I've got it under control.

I may say it's because I don't want to bother anyone, but the truth is, I don't want anyone to think I can't handle it. And if I am brutally honest, I want to look like a martyr. It feels like a rush of validation when you hear someone say, "I don't know how you are doing it all!" You feel like you have cracked the code, and you are winning. When you hear validation like, "I don't know how you do it all," that's the fuel hustle culture runs on.

Self-reliance is a survival skill, but it's not maintainable. Consider this: Wearing a coat when it's cold is smart because it keeps you warm; carrying it every day, even if it's 80°, just weighs you down. The cost of doing it all can make you resentful and so bogged down that you feel like you can't come up for air.

There are times during a crisis when resources are scarce or when no one else can step in. In these situations, self-reliance may be the only way to move forward. But at some point, self-reliance stops looking like resilience and begins to look like another version of the busy badge. Rebuilding requires something more, including support, space, and the courage to stop carrying everything alone.

TRADING YOUR BUSY BADGE FOR A QUALITY CROWN

Trading your busy badge for a quality crown starts with being honest about what your busyness is masking — your needs, your values, and things that might be waiting for you to pause long enough to see.

I used to believe that the fuller my calendar, the more meetings, and the later I worked, all proved I was successful. No matter what I did, hustle culture demanded more.

But I was using busyness to hide from my feelings and outrun my pain. If I didn't have time to feel it, surely it would go away. Eventually, I decided I didn't want to outrun my life. I want to live it. To do that, I asked myself these key questions:

- Is what I'm doing meaningful, or is it just filling space?
- Does this reflect my values or just my calendar?

When you choose quality over busyness, you will stop living on autopilot, and you can rebuild forward with intention. Quality is the lens that helps you move forward with clarity and intention to the life you want to live.

> *When you choose quality over busyness, you will stop living on autopilot, and you can rebuild forward with intention.*

REFLECTION:

Define Quality Time

Take a few quiet minutes and list the top five things filling your calendar.

Next to each one, write: "Meaningful" or "Just filling space."

Circle the one(s) you want to adjust or approach differently this week and think about how you can make it happen.

CHAPTER 12

Where Ritual Meets Healing

There was a time when grief had rituals and seasons, when mourning was seen and honored. Some believe emotions should be kept quiet, while others encourage public displays such as dancing or altars for the dead. Grief is a timeless human experience.

There are many ways to acknowledge grief, and your way doesn't have to look like anyone else's.

Too often, our world is moving too fast, and we praise resilience while rewarding productivity. Mourning any loss has become a private process and often involves red, blotchy eyes on Zoom and pretending everything is okay. We are left to create our own rituals in a world that has forgotten them, and we are expected to move on quickly.

Consider Queen Charlotte's famous line in the Netflix show *Bridgerton*: "Sorrows, sorrows, prayers,"[26] she would say in a rush to comfort someone, dismissing them. Today, we do the same; we pat a shoulder and offer the universal, "Sorry for your loss." Brushing someone off in this way — offering meaningless sympathy or not acknowledging it at all — makes them feel as if their pain is a burden.

When we acknowledge someone's grief with more than the standard reply but instead, with an authentic, heartfelt expression of sympathy, it feels like whispering in their ear that they don't have to carry it alone.

RECLAIMING RITUALS

Mourning isn't just for death and funerals. Divorce, job loss, infidelity, loss of the life we imagined, loss of identity, and many other losses also deserve to be acknowledged. Reclaiming rituals is a way to honor them. You have permission to create a ritual that can add structure to chaos, regardless of the disruption.

Consider creating your own rituals if your culture doesn't provide them. You get to decide what works best for you and what feels right. The suggestions below can be used for any script break, but before you read them, I want to emphasize: No ritual is silly or unnecessary. Rituals are intentional, meaningful pauses in a society that rarely gives time or space to rest and reset.

- Light a candle for anniversaries or significant days.
- Write a letter you won't send, giving yourself permission to say whatever you need.
- Create art or build something as a way of expression and remembrance.
- Keep a journal. This can be a memory journal, a health journal to track milestones and setbacks, or simply a daily journal where you free-write.

WHERE RITUAL MEETS HEALING

- Create a playlist of songs that bring you comfort, remind you of something or someone, or help you through challenging moments.
- Consider a symbolic gesture. After my dad passed, I started a memory rose garden. I have stepping stones to honor all my parents and in-laws, and the garden is filled with different types of roses in various colors.
- Create a memory album of your favorite photographs. When I can, I write my favorite memory on some of the photos so the stories will live on through generations.

There are countless more rituals you can try, and they don't have to be elaborate. What's important is that the ritual allows you to pause, reflect, remember milestones or transitions, and make time for yourself.

Whether ancient or created today, rituals can serve as reminders that we should not rush through grieving process. Loss deserves to be seen, felt, and honored in whatever way helps you rebuild forward.

What's Lost in Our Rush to "Move On"

Even with rituals that help us heal, many of us still rush through our pain. After every devastation, I have always felt an inherent drive to "move on and get over it." I've always smiled, pulled my shoulders back, and resumed business as usual.

While writing this book, I realized that no boss, colleague, family member, or friend ever handed me a stopwatch for grief. No one ever told me to hurry up. But somehow, I felt the pressure. Perhaps it stemmed from the emails filling up my inbox, the unspoken rules of the workplace, or the way some people avoided me so they wouldn't have to mention what happened.

Was I putting the pressure on myself, or was it society's script telling me to "be over it"? When I look at other cultures, it becomes even clearer how differently grief is honored elsewhere.

Grief Across Cultures

Around the world, grief doesn't always look like hushed voices and silent tears. Many cultures mourn "out loud" with vibrant festivals and rituals spent with loved ones and community. Some of their rituals take several days, supporting mourners by surrounding them with community and giving them the freedom to mourn without judgment.

- In Japan, families celebrate Obon each August — a time when it's believed the spirits of ancestors return home. Lanterns are lit in cemeteries, guiding loved ones back with a gentle, soft light. This celebration serves as a poignant reminder that those we love remain a part of our lives, even after they are gone.
- Mexico becomes vibrant with marigold flowers, sugar skulls, and favorite foods of the departed from October 31 to November 2 each year to celebrate the Day of the Dead. Families gather to celebrate, not to mourn.
- In Ghana, the Adowa Ceremony unites the community to honor the deceased through music, drumming, and dancing. Grief is openly expressed and not hidden away, as they celebrate the legacy of their loved ones.
- Tibetan Buddhists practice an ancient Buddhist ritual called Sky Burial, where the body of the deceased is returned to birds of prey to symbolize the return of the body to the natural cycle of life and death.[27]

While we may not have marigolds or lantern festivals, the principle is the same: Grief should be honored. The rituals and celebrations in Japan, Mexico, Ghana, and Tibet demonstrate that many cultures do not view grief as something to be experienced alone, silently, or quickly. In contrast, their rituals often last several days, allowing them to be with their community and mourn together.

While many of these traditions focus on death, the principles are true for other script breaks in life, including divorce, job loss, infertility, or any other disruption. These difficulties may not come with public ceremonies, but it's essential to create your own rituals that help you rebuild forward.

Collective Grieving

Collective grieving occurs when a community, nation, or group comes together in response to a loss. Instead of going through it alone, grief is shared. These moments are often ritualized: funerals, vigils, memorial services, and the structure is comforting. For many of us, being surrounded by others makes loss feel less isolating, and when sorrow is shared, it feels more bearable.

Collective grieving can look like:

- Public events, such as funerals, memorial services, and vigils
- National moments of silence or lowering flags
- Cultural practices like sitting shiva, wakes, or festivals

Collective grieving was a massive part of Queen Elizabeth's death. She passed away in 2022 after a 70-year reign, and her ceremonies were filled with rituals that not only celebrated her life and reign but also helped people mourn together. Her casket traveled from Balmoral Castle to public spaces across Scotland

and England before arriving at Westminster Hall, where people waited for hours to pay their respects. Soldiers carried her casket and placed it on a raised wooden platform where the imperial state crown, orb, and scepter were arranged meticulously.[28]

I watched the entire funeral of Queen Elizabeth. The streets were lined with people, gathered shoulder to shoulder, comforting each other. Even though I'm not British and she wasn't my queen, I still found myself grieving. I was in awe of the symbolism worked into every detail, from the attire to the music and procession, and I noted how it created a sense of unity and shared loss.

Collective grieving provides mourners with the opportunity to express their sorrow and feel supported. For many, the shared experience and empathy provide comfort, helping them process what has happened.

We have experienced rich and deeply meaningful collective grieving in the United States. After the terrorist attacks on September 11, 2001, the nation mourned together. Memorial services, vigils, and community gatherings took place across the country, allowing people to grieve together and support one another.

During COVID-19, collective grieving took on a new shape through social media. Mourning wasn't private anymore. It was something we could all share, even while physically apart. We will never forget watching people say goodbye to loved ones through hospital windows or over the phone. It was devastating. However, in that shared horror and fear, social media became a kind of ritual, giving us a way to grieve together and not feel that we were alone.

Moments like COVID-19 or the death of a public figure remind us that the Western world does have room for collective grieving, but those moments are rare. Here, grief is most often a private and individualized experience. We may have support for the funeral, but often, that's the only collective grieving our culture promotes. We aren't encouraged to mourn "out loud," but instead, to do it quietly, behind closed doors, so we don't bother anyone.

There isn't a "right" way to grieve, and I'm not suggesting that one way of grieving is better than another. Grief and loss are deeply personal, and no two people will experience them the same. Perhaps what we need is a space for both individual and collective practice, so every form of grief can be seen.

Grief in Literature

Just as rituals give us actions to hold onto, literature gives us words. Literature gives us permission to be honest about our grief and not hide from it or pretend it isn't happening. Although literature offers different perspectives, there is a singular truth: Grief doesn't care who you are, how busy you are, or how many days you can take off work. It demands to be felt and will only ease in its own time.

Grief has been part of storytelling since stories have existed. One of the earliest examples comes from around 2100 BCE, in a story called the *Epic of Gilgamesh*, preserved on clay tablets and discovered in the 1800s.[29] It's about a king devastated by the death of a friend and the universal pain of loss. Even thousands of years ago, humans were going through the same pain we do and asking themselves: What does it mean when someone we love dies?

In 1917, Sigmund Freud transitioned from his usual focus on dreams and sexuality to publish *Mourning and Melancholia*. Freud suggested that mourning is a natural and even necessary process, while melancholia, what we now call depression, happens in the unconscious mind and requires a different kind of care. His distinction between the two has helped shape how Western psychology discusses grief.[30]

While Freud analyzed grief scientifically, William Shakespeare wrote beautiful words about it in sonnets and plays. A prolific writer, Shakespeare grieved for many in his life, which became a theme in his work. His play, *Hamlet*, is about a son struggling with grief for his father, along with his anger at the injustice of his death. This play explores several themes of grief, including the enduring, natural, existential, pervasive, and relatable aspects.[31] Through his characters, Shakespeare showed that grief is universal and touches everyone, from kings to commoners.

C.S. Lewis wrote one of my husband Justin's favorite books, *A Grief Observed*, which is one of the most honest accounts of mourning ever published. When Lewis lost his wife after a long battle with cancer, he wrote about his pain, sorrow, and questions. This vulnerable book gave a glimpse into someone suffering with gut-wrenching sorrow.[32]

Justin teaches a course called *Faith and Reason* at Franklin College, a private liberal arts college in Indiana, and uses several C.S. Lewis texts. He reminded me that before *A Grief Observed*, Lewis wrote *The Problem of Pain*, an essay that tried to reconcile a good God with the existence of evil. Lewis explored questions of heaven and hell, the suffering of people and animals, and the random pain caused by nature itself. As Justin puts it, "It's a brilliant essay, but written from the comfort of Lewis's fairly comfortable life."

About *A Grief Observed*, Justin says, "This one isn't an essay. It's a journal Lewis wrote after his wife's death from cancer. Unlike the antiseptically clean *Problem of Pain*, written from a distance, *A Grief Observed* is written from the trenches of the anguish. Lewis is filled with anger, and he, one of the greatest Christian authors of all time, calls God a 'cosmic sadist' and an 'eternal vivisector.'"

Justin's favorite C.S. Lewis line in the book addresses the difference between intellectual belief and lived experience:

WHERE RITUAL MEETS HEALING

"It is easy to believe a rope to be strong and sound as long as you are merely using it to cord a box. But suppose that you had to hang by that rope over a precipice. Wouldn't you then first discover how much you really trusted it?"

"That's the difference," Justin told me, "between your trust in your values before and after a script break."

He went on to share that his students consistently rate *A Grief Observed* as one of the most meaningful texts in his class. He said, "As an intellectual experience, nothing beats *Reasonable Faith* (a text written by Dr. William Lane Craig outlining philosophical arguments for the existence of God), but life isn't about intellect alone; it's also about experience. *A Grief Observed* wins their hearts because it shows them they aren't alone in their loss. No amount of theory can insulate us from the truest script break, losing someone we love."

Lewis showed that even faith and intellect can crumble under the weight of loss, and his honesty gives generations permission to speak their pain. Today, that same courage echoes through works like Megan Devine's *It's OK That You're Not OK*, and Kate Spencer's *The Dead Moms Club*.

Kate Spencer's book[33] helped me after Mom died because she speaks so openly and honestly about grief. My husband and I had planned a vacation that happened to fall a week after she passed. The hotel we stayed in featured a world-class spa with a wide range of amenities, including a reading area with private nooks equipped with book lights and curtains for added privacy. I went early to my treatment so I could enjoy the space. I changed into my robe, grabbed a fuzzy blanket, settled into one of the private nooks, and immersed myself in the book. Even after my treatment, I returned to my cozy nook to keep reading. I read through laughter and tears and found myself feeling truly *seen* by someone. Kate's vulnerability helped me not to feel so alone in my grief.

That afternoon in the spa reinforced in me that grief needs acknowledgement, expression, and room to breathe. Whether through rituals, shared mourning, or literature, every ritual allows you to move through loss instead of around it.

REFLECTION:

A Ritual Of Your Own

Take a moment to consider a loss or script break that you have experienced.

1. Consider a script break you haven't fully acknowledged.
2. Write one sentence about what it changed for you.
3. Choose a small ritual that feels meaningful to you (lighting a candle, taking a walk, making a playlist, journaling, writing a letter, etc.).
4. Commit and schedule when you'll practice the ritual this week.

PART 4

REBUILD FORWARD

CHAPTER 13

Living Your Values

You hit reset, called it like it was, got back to you, dared to dream, and are rewriting your new script. Now it's time to live it. In chapter 6, Get Back to You, you rediscovered your core identity. This chapter is about what comes next and how you can align your daily choices, relationships, and routines with your new values.

Psychologist Ryan C. Warner notes that when our goals and behaviors line up with our internal purpose, we experience greater well-being, resilience, and motivation.[34] When we're out of alignment, it can show up quietly as tension, fatigue, or a nagging feeling that something is off. Over time, that wears you down, even if everything looks fine on the outside.

Close your eyes and imagine what your life would look like if it were aligned. Would it bring calm, energy, or both? You may find that you now define success differently than you once did.

You're not abandoning your old self; you're evolving into a fuller version of who you've always been. You can build a life that not only looks right on the outside but feels true on the inside.

WHAT SURVIVED THE BREAK

When Mom died seven months after Dad, everything that was familiar disappeared. During that season, I realized how fortunate I was to have had parents who loved me so much and a husband who jumped right in to support me, both physically and emotionally. I could feel my parents' values in my brother (uncle) and a nephew (cousin), and we make a tight-knit, three-pack family. It was during this season that I realized I also needed to show up for myself.

Many of my old values, such as loyalty, hard work, and achievement, were inherited. However, not all of them served me well. That didn't mean I wasn't still loyal, and I still valued work and achievement. It meant that my values needed to be refined to fit who I had become. I also had to release values that weren't really mine to begin with, such as needing to please others, keeping my emotions to myself, equating productivity with worth, always saying yes, or focusing solely on keeping everyone happy. Those expectations were handed down from culture, family, and the workplace, but they came at a cost.

Who Shows Up

When you are going through the worst moments of your life, you will notice who surrounds you. Who are the ones standing beside you, checking in, and offering to help? My best friend, Andrea, was there every step of the way, even helping clean out my parents' house. Our relationship grew because she checked on me daily, offering endless support, encouragement, and love.

I always thought of myself as having lots of friends. I typically get along well with everyone and consider myself easy to get along with. Grief changed the lens through which I looked. I began to notice that many people I once considered close didn't come around when I needed them the most, while others showed up in unexpected ways, such as dropping off dinner, running errands, or driving three and a half hours to attend funerals.

I wasn't angry at those who didn't show up; I was too overwhelmed to think about it much. As the fog lifted, I began to see that my values had shifted, and I needed friendships that reflected those values. I wanted to surround myself with people who showed up authentically, consistently, and with empathy, fitting with the values I was now living by.

There was no confrontation or dramatic ending. I still care for them and wish them well. Perhaps my script breaks triggered them; grief can stir up things people aren't ready to face. We don't always know what someone else is carrying. I can give them grace and be there if they ever need me, while still giving myself permission to reorder my relationships.

My high-value friendships — the ones that align with where I am now — are where I invest the most time and energy. The others remain part of my life, but with boundaries. It's not rejection; it's realignment.

My high-value friendships — the ones that align with where I am now — are where I invest the most time and energy. The others remain part of my life, but with boundaries. It's not rejection; it's realignment.

REDEFINING WHAT REALLY MATTERS

Your values are the blueprint for rebuilding. After my script broke, I began to notice the small but significant ways my values had changed. The values that once guided me no longer felt urgent or accurate. They didn't change overnight; they evolved slowly and quietly, as life reminded me of what really mattered. Here are a few notable shifts:

- **From perfection to presence**
  I used to spend a lot of my time maintaining what I thought was a perfect image. This included a clean house, home-cooked dinners, and the best put-together version of myself I could present. But after loss and grief, keeping all of it up felt exhausting, unfulfilling, and irrelevant. I realized that takeout fills your belly, too, and a few dishes in the sink or a little dust on the shelves wouldn't hurt anyone.

  I still showed up at work and performed well, even when I was makeup-free. What mattered instead was spending time with family and friends who shared my values.

- **From saving for "someday" to living for today**
  I was raised to be a saver, and for years, I took pride in being frugal. After the losses, I learned that "someday" can disappear in the blink of an eye. I still value financial responsibility, but now I'm intentional about making space for experiences that bring joy and connection.

  In 2024, I splurged on Justin Timberlake tickets. I attended three concerts in three different cities with my husband and son. Each trip was full of laughter, music, and memories we'll carry with us forever. When I posted photos, a few people made comments about the cost — "must be nice" — and for a moment, I felt guilty. Then I remembered, alignment means letting go of other people's opinions.

  These trips weren't about excess. They were about joy, presence, and soaking up moments with the people I love (plus seeing my lifelong crush on stage).

  Sometimes it's more important to fill your soul than your savings account.

  Sometimes it's more important to fill your soul than your savings account.

- **From screening calls to answering with intention**
  I used to be queen of screening calls, telling myself I was too busy and would return the call later. After losing people I loved, I realized what a gift it is when someone reaches out. Now, when the phone rings, I answer.

  What an honor it is to be thought of. Those moments of connection and the voice on the other end of the line are what truly matter.

Your value shifts will look different than mine, but the principle is the same: disruption clarifies. It strips away what doesn't matter so you can see what does. Living in alignment begins by noticing what no longer fits and having the courage to choose what does.

> *Living in alignment begins by noticing what no longer fits and having the courage to choose what does.*

Putting Alignment into Practice

I still have moments when anxiety catches me off guard. Panic attacks aren't as frequent as they once were, but they still happen. The difference lies in how I view them. Instead of being frustrated with myself, I use them as a sign to stop, pause, and realign.

Alignment isn't about perfection; it's about consistency and choosing, again and again, to live in a way that honors who you've now become. Some days it feels easier to hold to your boundaries and take care of yourself. Other days fall apart before you've had your

> *Alignment isn't about perfection; it's about consistency and choosing, again and again, to live in a way that honors who you've now become.*

first cup of coffee. When that happens, be gentle with yourself and use these moments to course-correct — say no to an extra meeting, apologize when you are short with someone, or give yourself grace when the day doesn't go as planned.

Alignment is a practice, not a destination. It requires constant small adjustments. I used to push through exhaustion to finish everything on my list. Now I know that sometimes the most aligned choice is to rest and pick it back up tomorrow.

REFLECTION:

Practicing Alignment

You can start practicing alignment by checking in with yourself throughout the day. Ask yourself questions like:

- Does this choice reflect my values?
- Am I doing this out of obligation?
- Have I decided to do this because I am worried?
- Am I acting intentionally, or am I acting under pressure?
- What would bring me peace at this moment?

As you ask these questions, you'll start noticing patterns — what drains you, what restores you, and what truly feels like you. Alignment grows through attention. It's not built in the big moments, but in the everyday choices that allow you to shape a life that feels like yours again.

CHAPTER 14

Rebuilding That Works for You

Eventually, you'll reach a moment when your past definition of success stops fitting the person you have become. This chapter is about that moment and how to find a rhythm that works for the life you are living now.

The hardest part of rebuilding isn't starting over; it's realizing the life that once worked no longer fits. Sometimes that realization arrives like a crash. Other times it's a quiet whisper that grows louder each day: *This isn't working anymore.* You tell yourself to be grateful. You've checked all the boxes, after all, but gratitude can't drown out truth.

When disruption breaks your routine, it exposes more than broken systems; it exposes broken rhythms. The way you've been working no longer matches who you've become. I'm not suggesting you quit your job or change your career trajectory or even launch a new business (though you might do all these things!). But you can begin rebuilding your relationship with work itself. The habits that once helped you survive may not help you thrive. It's time to create a rhythm that fits the life you are living now.

DISRUPTION REVEALS WHAT'S UNSUSTAINABLE

When we're on the other side of disruption, it's tempting to tell ourselves the best solution is to start over. Dr. Margaretha M. explains in her piece, "Why Rebuilding After a Major Life Change is a Better Investment than Starting Over," that reinvention can imply your past has no value and that you have to become someone entirely new to move forward.

In reality, she writes, "Reconstruction acknowledges a fundamental truth that reinvention ignores: you already have the building blocks for your next chapter."[35] Your previous chapter has built who you are, and it's important to honor and respect what you've been through and what's led to your change.

You don't need to erase the old you to become the new you. After all, you are rebuilding forward, keeping the parts that still stand, repairing what cracked, and rebuilding something that works for you. Dr. Margaretha sums it up beautifully: "Your next chapter doesn't require becoming someone else; it calls for becoming more fully yourself."

BUILDING AND REBUILDING

Nearly fifteen years ago, my husband and I built our current home. Given Justin's disability, we needed several modifications, including lower countertops and cabinets (Justin is five feet tall), handicap rails, and wide hallways for when he uses his wheelchair. It was also just the two of us, since infertility altered our plans for a family.

We built a two-bedroom home with a handicap tub, no steps to climb, and a small fenced-in yard for our miniature schnauzer, Phoebe. We poured everything we had into this house, believing it was our forever home.

Fast forward to today. We have a teenager, two dogs, and a cat we inherited from Jan. Our house feels a lot more crowded. Our office was built for Justin, but now that I work from home, we have crammed two desks into the space. Our spare bedroom and the guest bathroom, which we previously used to host family and friends, became Christian's room and bathroom. Our bonus room upstairs, once used for storage, has been transformed into a gaming/friend hangout space for Christian, equipped with a couch, TV, and gaming computer.

When Jan moved in with us, we sold our dining room table to make space, transforming our dining room into a bedroom. Our once perfectly sized fenced-in yard now barely fits our two rambunctious goldendoodles, and our enclosed back porch has now become my art studio. Our home has been redesigned to suit our needs, and we are grateful.

However, all these changes are prompting us to consider building a new home for our expanding family. We want to make sure we have room to entertain. Perhaps we will need an extra bedroom or two, if Christian expands his family, two small offices, and a big backyard for pets.

Life changes over the years, and so do your needs. You've faced script breaks, perhaps a breakup, becoming an empty-nester, or a health shift that makes it necessary for you to rebuild. It's important to recognize when the shift happens and act on it.

You aren't rebuilding from scratch, but with intention. You keep what worked from the old house — the solid foundation, rooms filled with memories, your favorite reading chair — and you design something that fits your life now. You aren't demolishing your past; you are redesigning it for who you are today.

Old Definition of Success

We are taught that success is measured by outcomes — productivity, achievement, and approval. To be successful, we're told to chase the corner office, pack our calendar full of meetings, and somehow have time to do it all.

In every season of my life, success has been measured by outcomes. The specifics of what that success would look like have changed — like having a baby, climbing the proverbial career ladder, losing weight — but the message underneath has remained the same: Life will be better *once* I achieve the goal. There was always a finish line, but somehow it kept moving every time I reached it.

Each time I reached a goal, I felt pride for a few moments... and then it was on to the next goal or reflecting on what I should have done differently. I never allowed myself to celebrate; I was too focused on what came next. The less I celebrated myself, the less others did too.

For a long time, I thought this rhythm worked. If you looked at my LinkedIn, you would see my achievements listed: fundraising goals achieved, promotions, boards served on, and deadlines met. I presented my best self to the world, hiding the cracks.

But grief has a way of exposing what you are holding together with duct tape and popsicle sticks. I began to realize that I was hiding behind busyness and achievements. And I wasn't even stopping to celebrate achievements; I was just moving on to the next one.

I felt guilty when I had free time, comparing myself to others. If I had a free Saturday afternoon and saw someone else post on Facebook about how they were spending their Saturday volunteering, at a conference, or putting in extra hours at the office, I felt guilty. Rest felt like laziness, and stillness felt like failure.

It wasn't until the calendar was clear and the world was quiet that I had to face what I was hiding: exhaustion, disconnection, and the fear that I wasn't good enough without my accomplishments. It's a heavy dose to swallow. Sometimes the most productive thing you can do is pause. In fact, the more space I allow for stillness, the more present and creative I feel.

Pausing likely won't come naturally, and you may have to fight the urge to fill the space. But stillness doesn't mean you aren't productive. Instead, it means you are allowing yourself space, rest, and alignment. Once I stopped scheduling every hour, I could begin to redefine what success meant to me.

> *Rest felt like laziness, and stillness felt like failure.*

> *Sometimes the most productive thing you can do is pause.*

New Definition of Success

Now, success looks different. It needs to align with my passions and values. When I took the plunge and left my full-time job to start my speaking career and partner with my friend Dana in the consulting space, it was a dramatic departure from anything I had done before.

The shift began during a conversation with my mentor, Caroline. Together, we made a pro and con list of what it would mean to leave a salaried, full-time position with benefits to step into something uncertain but meaningful and exciting. I had built my career around stability and consistency, yet the more I looked at the list, the clearer it became that I wasn't looking for safety; I needed alignment.

The pros weren't just about opportunity; they reflected a new version of success. I needed meaningful work, flexibility, collaboration, and the chance to build something. I wasn't someone's assistant; I was now a business partner, shaping vision and strategy, not just supporting it.

My definition of success also changed when I became a mother. For fifteen years, it was just my husband and me. We had come to terms with being child-free and built a life around that reality. Then, when we adopted our nephew, everything shifted in an instant. My world, my priorities, and my sense of purpose realigned overnight.

I took a year off when we adopted Christian. Although he wasn't a baby, we had no idea what we were doing — we didn't even know where the middle school was! During that year, I took the lead on the long and emotional adoption process and did things like finding a pediatrician, dentist, and therapist, and enrolling him in school. I transformed our guest bedroom into a teenage boy's space with freshly painted walls, new bedding, a new bed, and his favorite posters.

Still, I wrestled with anxiety almost daily. I worried constantly about not working and what that meant for my identity and future. Even with my husband's reassurance that we were financially stable and that I needed to be home that first year, the guilt was relentless. I couldn't help but feel like I was falling behind. I continued to interview and apply for Salesforce positions, trying to prove, mostly to myself, that I was still "doing something." I didn't yet know how to measure my worth without a full calendar or paycheck.

WHAT SUCCESS LOOKS LIKE NOW

Something shifted once the adoption was finalized, and I realized success could no longer be measured by productivity alone. I was a mother, and success now looked like being *present*. Raising my son to be kind, respectful, and generous is the most important work I will ever do. It's not about what I can accomplish in a day; it's about making sure my son feels loved, supported, and safe.

Motherhood didn't lessen my ambition, but it reminded me of the kind of legacy I want to build: one that isn't measured in dollars or metrics, but in moments like watching movies, cheering him on at tennis, and having conversations at the end of the day. These are the moments that matter the most.

Success now feels quieter and more personal. I am paying attention to what makes me feel centered, calm, and appreciated. I give myself breaks in my schedule, and on days when I don't have back-to-back afternoon meetings, I will even take a nap without guilt.

Some things that now look like success to me are:

- A peaceful, calm morning without rushing
- Enjoying dinner with my family — even when it's takeout because the day got away from me
- Hearing laughter fill the room when my husband, son, and I play board games
- Letting go of my to-do list and having drinks with friends
- Taking my son to musicals and concerts, making lifelong memories
- Impromptu date nights with my husband, even when I had planned to clean the house or catch up on work
- Putting whatever I am doing down to answer my phone

This list will continue to evolve, just as I will. My definition of success has shifted from achievement to alignment, from doing to being.

When your life reflects your values, success isn't measured by what you accomplish. It's measured by how it feels to live it.

The Discomfort of Letting Go

It was harder than I expected to leave behind the familiar rhythm of coffee chatter with colleagues, a steady paycheck, an office, and benefits. The first morning I woke up feeling a mix of fear and excitement. It took me a few weeks to determine a new rhythm that fit my new life.

Letting go didn't just mean leaving a job; it meant breaking up with an identity. For years, I had been rewarded for being dependable, efficient, and available. Those were my currencies. When I stopped performing them, I wondered who I was without the applause. I began to understand that freedom can feel like fear at first. It's the same sensation, but the difference is direction.

I had spent my entire career supporting other people's priorities, and for the first time, I was shaping my own. My internal dialogue was filled with doubt, and questions swirled in my head. Was I disciplined enough to do this? Will I be successful? What if I fail? For so long, my achievements had been measured in numbers. How many emails did I answer? How many meetings were scheduled? How many people attended the event? How much money was raised? How many calls did I make?

What I eventually realized is that by letting go, I was creating space. I have created space for things I love, and that bring me joy. Now, I measure my days not just by output, but by how I feel. At the end of a long day, do I feel fulfilled? Happy? Excited? It's the answer to these questions that makes me feel successful.

NEW RHYTHMS

Starting your own business comes with its own pressure, but being in control of your work and life is a gift.

Most mornings begin with my new rhythm. After my husband and teenager head out the door. I sit with my two dogs and savor a quiet cup of coffee before we head out for a quick walk. That time outdoors clears my head and allows me to enter my day with intention.

I am genuinely excited for the work I do now. I get to collaborate with a variety of clients whose missions inspire me, and I measure impact not in emails or metrics, but in meaning. I would never have had the space to write this book without redefining what success looks like. Each time Dana and I complete a project that makes a difference, I feel proud, not just because it went well, but because the work itself matters.

Even with this new definition of success, I still have to remind myself not to slip back into old habits. The pull to overwork and overcommit is strong. The difference is that now I notice it sooner, and I know how to reset.

I still catch myself slipping into old patterns and rhythms, including the impulse to say "yes" no matter how busy I am, checking email one more time when out to dinner, and equating productivity with value. But now I catch myself, and I am working to live a more aligned life.

New, healthy rhythms for me include mid-morning walks with my dogs, stopping work for half an hour when my son gets home to hear about his day, and sitting a little longer with my cat when she is purring uncontrollably while lying on my lap. The work will still be there when I get up.

Boundaries aren't barriers; they are rhythms. I am replacing guilt with purpose. Rebuilding your relationship with work is a lifelong practice. Some seasons will pull you back toward old habits, but what's important is that you notice when your rhythm starts to feel off again and correct course.

For me, fulfillment doesn't come from doing more but from doing what matters. There will always be deadlines, meetings, and stress, but there's also creativity and presence. The rhythm you choose becomes the life you build, one ordinary moment at a time.

> *The rhythm you choose becomes the life you build, one ordinary moment at a time.*

REFLECTION:

What Will Your New Rhythm Be?

While sitting in stillness or taking a pause, reflect on your current rhythms. Are they working for you?

Take time to answer these questions to help you rebuild in a way that honors who you are *now*, not who you were *before*.

- Where do you feel like your rhythm is off?
- What would success look like if it didn't come with pressure?
- What part of your old story deserves to come with you, and what can you leave behind?

CHAPTER 15

You Don't Have to Go Back to Who You Were Before

> *The time will come*
> *when, with elation,*
> *You will greet yourself arriving*
> *at your own door, in your own mirror,*
> *and each will smile at the other's welcome.*
>
> —DEREK WALCOTT, LOVE AFTER LOVE

These lines capture the quiet miracle of rediscovery, the moment you realize that the person you've been searching for has been waiting inside you all along. This final chapter is where momentum meets meaning. It's about realizing the point was never to return to your old self, but to rebuild forward to who you are becoming.

There is a moment after loss when you stop searching for your old self and start thinking about who you've been underneath the pain and loss. For a while, you will try to reconnect with the old you. You may think that if you can get back to the old version of yourself, you will begin to feel normal.

But eventually, you will realize that things have shifted and so have you. You've become a blend of the past and present.

People mean well when they say, "You're getting back to your old self." The world pressures you to bounce back, get over it, and get back to normal. But what if that version of you no longer fits? Perhaps that version of you belonged to a different season, one that has served its purpose.

It's time to step into your new identity with peace, not pressure.

RESTORATION VS. REBUILDING

We often think of rebuilding as restoration, as if we are putting a house back together, brick by brick. But rebuilding means creating something new.

I grew up in a tiny village in Southern Illinois with fewer than fifty people. Every spring brought the threat of tornadoes. Our family had a basement, but after an earthquake years earlier, a crack in the foundation caused it to leak. When we heard the tornado sirens, we'd grab our emergency kit (with medications and important documents) and our pets, and head for the safest location in town: the church. On a good Sunday, that church might have twenty people attending, but it was the hub during tornadoes. The basement held nearly the whole town, and we'd gather with our pets, flashlights, and food people brought "just in case."

Sometimes the storm would pass quickly, and those nights were fun with neighbors catching up. On other nights, it was scary. One spring, a tornado approached the church where we were gathered. The adults turned all the tables on their sides and huddled the kids behind them. I remember being crouched behind a table, listening to the storm bear down on us — the freight train roar you can only believe once you've heard it yourself. The tornado split into two and narrowly missed the church, tearing through nearby towns. It was a terrifying night.

When the storm finally passed, the damage was widespread — sheds and garages were torn apart, trees were uprooted, and porches, pools, and trampolines were destroyed. The tornado even dropped off a few cows in our neighborhood! They were alive and well, just disoriented (who wouldn't be?). We repaired and rebuilt what we could and helped our neighbors do the same.

When we all pitched in to help our neighbors, the work wasn't always perfect. Shingles or siding might have ended up a slightly different color, and fences were often mended with a different type of wood. Yard furniture was put back in different places, and some things were just never found.

We couldn't rebuild things to look exactly the same, but that is what rebuilding forward means: honoring what was, while accepting that some things will always look different. Rebuilding wasn't about erasing the damage or pretending the storm hadn't happened. It was about mending what mattered most and learning to live with what had changed. It's the same in life; why try to mend something all the way back to the way it was before?

ACKNOWLEDGEMENT AND GRATITUDE

The woman I used to be got me through some of life's most difficult script breaks. She showed up for everyone: her parents, in-laws, husband, son, friends, and colleagues. She kept things moving when everything around her was falling apart. She did the best she could with the tools she had.

I don't want to be her again, but I am grateful for her. If it weren't for her, I wouldn't be the person I am today. Now, it's time for her to take a well-earned break.

Learning to trust the new version of yourself can feel a lot like letting someone else take the wheel. They no longer teach driver's ed in the high schools, so when Christian turned fifteen, we enrolled him in the local driving school to obtain his learner's permit. Then it was up to us to teach him behind the wheel. He needed 50 hours of driving time, including 10 hours at night. Justin was in charge of teaching him, while I sat in the backseat.

Trust grew in small steps. We started with short drives around town, before transitioning to longer, more difficult drives. Every time we were in the car — whether Christian was driving or he was riding with us — Justin and I were modeling, instructing, and protecting. Slowly, we eased up and allowed him to take control.

When he turned sixteen and a half, he passed the exam and obtained his driver's license. Of course, I was a little fearful at first and had to fight the urge to grab the wheel. It's a lot like the fear you might feel when you let your old self step aside.

It's not a lack of confidence in what he was taught — I trust that what Justin and I gave him is enough. That's what I am asking you to do with your old identity: Thank that version for what you learned, trust what was built, and know it's safe for you to take the wheel yourself.

RELEASE AND EMERGENCE

You aren't erasing who you were; you are loosening your grip on the version of you that was created to survive. Forgive yourself for what you didn't know and the ways you stayed in survival mode — perhaps longer than you needed to. You are freeing yourself to live differently.

It was only after I released the old version of myself that I realized I'd been holding my breath. During yoga one morning, I noticed it: I'd been holding my breath to hold everything else together. When I finally exhaled, I gave myself permission to move forward without fixing everything first, to rebuild from right where I was.

MY REBUILDING

I've never been afraid to take a calculated risk. I think things through carefully, weighing the pros and cons, and once I make a decision, I act on it. Fear has never stopped me from taking the next step, although life's detours have often rewritten the plan.

Like you, I've had my share of script breaks: the loss of my biological parents and the grandparents who became my parents, infertility struggles, the deaths of my in-laws, adopting my son at twelve, and caring for my husband through years of surgeries and pain. Each loss has carried me toward a new beginning.

Looking back, I realize my rebuilds have been connected by resilience, persistence, and a willingness to begin again.

In my early years, I thought I'd work in medicine. Then came banking, administration, communications, and fundraising. Each role taught me something different: how to listen, adapt, and tell a story that mattered. My career hasn't been a straight shot. It's had lots of bends in the road that kept testing and teaching me.

When I married Justin and moved for his doctorate, I started over again at the Indiana University Foundation. There, I discovered my love of connecting purpose and people. While balancing graduate school and work at Franklin College, I discovered new interests in building programs and events, and I realized how much I loved telling the stories of students, professors, and alumni.

Motherhood was the most personal rediscovery. Adopting our son taught me patience and vulnerability. It also taught me to consider what really matters.

Caregiving for Jan deepened that lesson by making me redefine what strength really meant. When she died and the fog of caregiving lifted, I had space to think about what I wanted next. Partnering with Dana in the consulting space and stepping into my speaking and writing career was the first time I rebuilt by choice, not necessity. I wake up excited to create something that aligns with who I've become, not by discarding the past, but rather by carrying forward what is worth keeping and releasing what isn't.

Your rebuild won't look like mine. It will come from your experiences — what you choose to carry forward and what you decide to release. Don't measure your story against anyone else's.

You don't have to go back to who you were.

You've already become someone new.

REBUILDING FORWARD

All the script breaks in our lives deserve to be acknowledged and felt — the visible ones, like death, job loss, divorce, or the loss of a beloved pet, as well as the invisible ones, like the loss of a dream or the life you imagined. Every loss deserves space and to be seen.

Over these pages, you've moved through the five steps of the Momentum Method: Hit Reset, Call It Like It Is, Get Back to You, Dare to Dream, and Rewrite Your Script. It's important to remember that rebuilding forward isn't a linear journey;

you'll revisit these steps again and again, and each time you'll know more about yourself. Some days, you will feel as though you've lost momentum, and that's okay. One step back doesn't erase your progress.

Just keep returning to yourself, again and again.

Focus on momentum, moving ahead one choice, one chapter, and one breath at a time. And remember: You don't bounce back — you rebuild forward.

Focus on momentum, moving ahead one choice, one chapter, and one breath at a time. And remember: You don't bounce back — you rebuild forward.

Endnotes

1. Rebecca Schneid, "What Are 'the Twisties' in Gymnastics? Simone Biles Faced the Condition at the Tokyo Olympics," *Time*, August 1, 2024. https://time.com/7004666/what-are-the-twisties-gymnastics-cause-treatments-simone-biles-condition/.
2. Ann Curry, interview by Kate Coyne, *People*, January 16, 2018.
3. Deborah Norville Went Through 'a Major Depression' After Leaving 'Today' in 1991 (Exclusive)," *People.com*.
4. Michelle Williams, interview by Chris Heath, *GQ*, February 2012.
5. Sandberg, Sheryl, and Adam Grant. *Option B: Facing Adversity, Building Resilience, and Finding Joy*. New York: Alfred A. Knopf, 2017.
6. Andrew Garfield, interview by Stephen Colbert, *The Late Show with Stephen Colbert*, CBS, November 22, 2021.
7. Wondermind, "Our Story," *Wondermind*, accessed October 8, 2025, https://www.wondermind.com/our-story/.
8. Robbins, Mel. *The 5 Second Rule: Transform Your Life, Work, and Confidence with Everyday Courage*. New York: Savio Republic, 2017.
9. Janet M. Ruane, Ph.D., and Karen A. Cerulo, Ph.D., "How We Dream of Our Future," *Psychology Today* (blog), May 18, 2022, https://www.psychologytoday.com/us/blog/the-future-you/202205/how-we-dream-our-future.

10 *Odyssey Plans: What is an Odyssey Plan?* YouTube video, 1:23, Stanford Life Design Lab, April 7, 2024, https://youtu.be/wnU5DaIPr2Q.

11 Oprah Winfrey, *Academy of Achievement*, accessed November 24, 2025, https://achievement.org/achiever/oprah-winfrey/.

12 Viola Davis Opens Up About Growing Up Poor: 'There's a Lot of Shame Involved with Poverty,'" *EEW Magazine Online*, December 8, 2020, https://www.eewmagazineonline.com/featured/2020/12/8/viola-davis-opens-up-about-growing-up-poor-theres-a-lot-of-shame-involved-with-poverty.

13 Holly Hexter, "As Actress Viola Davis' Star Soars, Others Recall Upward Bound Beginnings," *Council for Opportunity in Education*, January 3, 2017, https://coenet.org/news-impact/blog/as-actress-viola-davis-star-soars-others-recall-upward-bound-beginnings/.

14 Tyler Perry Discusses Being Molested and His Traumatic Childhood," *Oprah.com*, accessed November 24, 2025, https://www.oprah.com/oprahshow/tyler-perry-discusses-being-molested--his-traumatic-childhood.

15 Hadley Freeman, "Tyler Perry: 'All My Life I've Been Called the N-Word,'" *The Guardian*, April 3, 2009, https://www.theguardian.com/film/2009/apr/03/tyler-perry-comedy-black-entertainment.

16 Sarah Wilson, "The Meaning of Life Scripts," *The Guardian*, March 8, 2009, https://www.theguardian.com/lifeandstyle/2009/mar/08/life-scripts.

17 Dr. M Pogosyan, "Why It Helps to Put Your Feelings Into Words," *Psychology Today*, September 23, 2021, https://www.psychologytoday.com/us/blog/between-cultures/202109/why-it-helps-to-put-your-feelings-into-words.

18 I Am Sober. (2024, January 23). *Robert Downey Jr on addiction*. I Am Sober. https://iamsober.com/en/blog/robert-downey-jr-sober-story.

ENDNOTES

19 T. White, "Robert Downey Jr's Redemption Story: The Stuff of Hollywood Miracles," *iNews*, March 11, 2024, https://inews.co.uk/culture/film/robert-downey-jrs-redemption-story-stuff-hollywood-miracles-2949824.

20 *theGrio*. "Tracee Ellis Ross: Actress, Entrepreneur and Advocate for Empowerment." April 21, 2025. https://thegrio.com/2025/04/21/tracee-ellis-ross/.

21 (Mayer, K. (2024, June 28). "Why employers need to step up on bereavement benefits." SHRM. https://www.shrm.org/topics-tools/news/benefits-compensation/why-employers-need-to-step-up-on-bereavement-benefits).

22 (2024, May 14) "Divorce's impact on work productivity." Hello Divorce. https://hellodivorce.com/expenses/divorces-impact-on-work-productivity).

23 Vivian Ching, PhD. "Social Identity Theory." *The Decision Lab.* Accessed September 23, 2025. https://thedecisionlab.com/reference-guide/psychology/social-identity-theory.

24 Ray Williams, "Are You Addicted to Busyness?" *Medium*, April 4, 2022, https://raybwilliams.medium.com/are-you-addicted-to-busyness-3a08ced87cb8.

25 Wang, Monica L. "Research: Why Employees Work While Sick—and How Leaders Can Stop It." *Harvard Business Review*, June 3, 2025. https://hbr.org/2025/06/research-why-employees-work-while-sick-and-how-leaders-can-stop-it.

26 Korrapati, Sathya. "What 'Sorrows, Sorrows, Prayers' Really Means in *Queen Charlotte: A Bridgerton Story*." *Business Insider*, May 14, 2023. https://www.businessinsider.com/queen-charlotte-bridgerton-sorrows-sorrows-prayers-meaning-explained-2023-5.

27 Clear Cremations. 2024. "How Do Different Cultures from Around the World Deal with Death?" *Clear Cremations.* Accessed September 29, 2025. https://clearcremations.com/how-do-different-cultures-from-around-the-world-deal-with-death/.

28 Reader's Digest, "Queen Elizabeth's Funeral: The Details and Traditions," *Reader's Digest,* November 29, 2023, https://www.rd.com/article/queen-elizabeth-royal-funeral/.

29 Ira Spar, "Gilgamesh," *Heilbrunn Timeline of Art History,* The Metropolitan Museum of Art, April 1, 2009, https://www.metmuseum.org/essays/gilgamesh.

30 Carhart-Harris, Robin L., Helen S. Mayberg, Andrea L. Malizia, and David Nutt. "Mourning and Melancholia Revisited: Correspondences between Principles of Freudian Metapsychology and Empirical Findings in Neuropsychiatry." *Annals of General Psychiatry* 7, no. 9 (July 24, 2008). https://doi.org/10.1186/1744-859X-7-9.

31 wordynerdbird. 2021. "Shakespeare's 'Hamlet': A Study of Grief." *Shakespeare Nerd,* July 15, 2021. https://shakespearenerd.home.blog/2021/07/15/hamlet-grief/.

32 Lindsley, Arthur W. 2001. "C.S. Lewis on Grief." *C.S. Lewis Institute,* December 5, 2001. https://www.cslewisinstitute.org/resources/c-s-lewis-on-grief/.

33 Kate Spencer, *The Dead Moms Club: A Memoir About Death, Grief, and Surviving the Mother of All Losses* (Boston: Seal Press, 2017).

34 Ryan C. Warner, "Living in Alignment With Values, Identity, and Purpose," *Psychology Today,* June 2, 2025, accessed October 4, 2025, https://www.psychologytoday.com/us/blog/leadership-diversity-and-wellness/202506/living-in-alignment-with-values-identity-and-purpose).

35 M, Margaretha. "Why Rebuilding after a Major Life Change Is a Better Investment than Starting Over," *LinkedIn.* Accessed October 17, 2025. https://www.linkedin.com/pulse/why-rebuilding-after-major-life-change-better-than-starting-montagu-8wqxf/.

Acknowledgements

To my husband, Justin — You've seen me at my best and my most undone, and you've loved me through all of it. You've stood beside me through every script break and every rebuild, carrying the weight with me and cheering for every dream. I am endlessly grateful for your love, humor, and belief in me, especially on the days I couldn't find it myself. I love you to the moon and back.

To my son, Christian — Thank you for believing in me with your whole heart and for giving me the joy of watching you grow into such an incredible young man. I am so lucky to be your mom and am so proud of you. You remind me every day why rebuilding forward matters.

To my brother, Mark — Thank you for your unwavering support, for believing I can do anything I set my mind to, and for the wisdom and perspective you always bring when I need it the most. I'm especially grateful you chose to share your story in this book. It means the world to me.

To my nephew, Keith — Thank you for your steady support and belief in me through all the seasons of life.

To my best friend and chosen sister, Andrea — There is no one who has walked more closely beside me through every twist, setback, and breakthrough. Your friendship is one of the greatest gifts of my life.

To my mentor, Caroline — No one believes in me quite like you do. Every dream I've brought to you, you've helped me bring to life, including this book. Thank you for your wisdom, your encouragement, and for teaching me to honor my own voice. I am humbled and honored that you wrote the foreword. Your words set the tone for this book, and your faith in me has shaped far more than these pages.

To Dana, my friend and colleague — Thank you for welcoming me into a partnership where my strengths are seen, valued, and trusted. I'm grateful for your friendship, collaboration, and for sharing your story in the book.

To Katie and Emily, who also shared their stories — Thank you for your courage, vulnerability, and trust. Your openness brought this book to life, and I am forever grateful for your friendship and honesty.

To the Niche Press team, who guided me every step of the way — Thank you for helping me take my idea and turn it into a book I am incredibly proud of. Your partnership, patience, and expertise made this dream possible.

To all my friends who cheered me on, supported me, and stood beside me during the script breaks, the aftermath, and the rebuild: You've helped me hold on when I couldn't see the way forward.

And finally, to you, the reader — Thank you for picking up this book. My hope is that it meets you where you are in your own story. When the world tells you to bounce back, I hope you instead choose to rebuild forward, on your terms, in your time, and with your whole heart.

About Andrea Gash

Andrea Gash is a sought-after speaker, facilitator, career coach, and author who believes you don't bounce back — you rebuild forward. With a background in communications and strategic leadership, Andrea brings both heart and practicality to her work, helping individuals rebuild after life's script breaks: loss, career shifts, identity changes, or when life doesn't go as planned.

Through her workshops, keynotes, and coaching, Andrea offers actionable tools for moving forward with clarity and confidence, including her signature five-step Momentum Method, a framework for rebuilding after disruption. Her approach blends professional expertise with lived experience, having navigated her own seasons of loss, resilience, and rebuilding.

A keynote speaker and facilitator in the higher education, nonprofit, and corporate sectors, Andrea is known as an Activation Speaker who leaves audiences inspired to put ideas into action. She has been featured on national podcasts, webinars, and at industry conferences.

Andrea holds a bachelor's degree in communications from the University of Southern Indiana and a master's degree in strategic communications from Purdue University.

When she isn't speaking or coaching, Andrea enjoys yoga, oil painting, and starting her day with a strong cup of coffee. She treasures time with her husband, their son, and her two dogs, who remind her daily that joy often hides in ordinary moments.

Her core belief — and the heart of her book — is simple: No matter what breaks, you can always rebuild and move forward.

CONTACT

Website: AndreaGash.com
Email: Andrea@AndreaGash.com
LinkedIn: LinkedIn.com/in/AndreaGash

www.ingramcontent.com/pod-product-compliance
Lightning Source LLC
LaVergne TN
LVHW021339080526
838202LV00004B/228